Assisting
the
Traumatized
Soul

Assisting the Traumatized Soul

Healing the Wounded Talisman

by Phyllis K. Peterson

Bahá'í Publishing Trust
Wilmette, Illinois

Bahá'í Publishing Trust, Wilmette, Illinois 60091-2844

Copyright © 1999 by the National Spiritual Assembly of the
Bahá'ís of the United States
All Rights Reserved. Published 1999
Printed in the United States of America

02   01   00   99   4   3   2   1

Library of Congress Cataloging-in-Publication Data

Peterson, Phyllis, 1941–
    Assisting the traumatized soul : healing the wounded
    talisman/by Phyllis Peterson.
              p.   cm.
    Includes bibliographical references and index.
    ISBN 0-87743-274-0
    1. Bahai Faith.   2. Spiritual healing.   3. Peterson,
Phyllis, 1941–.   4. Adult child sexual abuse victims—
Religious life.   I. Title.
BP377.P48   1998
297.9'3442—dc21   98-29170
                                                  CIP

Original Cover Art by Jaki Craske
Cover Design by Scott Hammond, D&S Graphics

*T*o my mother, Kathryn Albano Taylor, who is my model for the qualities of generosity, humor, courage, sacrifice, and service as a handmaiden of God. She taught me to protect and care for those who need an advocate. She taught me to never give up during tests and difficulties. She taught me that I could survive any injustice, any depression, any trial, as long as I turned to God and believed in myself. I am grateful to her that she held our family together with every ounce of strength that she had. This one act is the greatest miracle of my childhood.

This then will be a key permitting one to enter places the gates to which were locked. And when these gates are opened and these places are entered into, the soul will find rest therein, the eyes will be delighted, and the bodies will be eased of their toil and of their labor.

—*Maimonides*

Table of Contents

Acknowledgments

I have been carried forward in my quest to write this book by many people; and I wish to thank them for their support. Foremost on this long list is my husband, John Peterson, who ungrudgingly gave up his rights to the computer and encouraged me to write. I also wish to thank Kathy Roesch and Stig Karlberg for that all-important "first Fireside" I attended in 1969; homefront pioneers Margaret and the late Ed Clayton for their perseverance in teaching the Cause to me and to multitudes of others; Cathy Wolfe, whose knowledge of the Bahá'í Writings was extremely valuable to me; Calvin Thomas, who introduced me to John Bradshaw; Donna Carter, who was instrumental in connecting me with the Parent Action Network; Ann Natale, who sees me when I don't see myself and is therefore in a position to advocate to me for me; Steven B. Zwickel, author of *All the Rage,* who influenced me to study anger; Sally Casper, Executive Director of the Wisconsin Committee for the Prevention of Child Abuse, who helped me believe in my creativity; my mother, Kathryn Taylor, who taught me to never give up; my children, Nancy, Cynthia, and Curtis, who inspire me, as youth is prone to, to follow them fearlessly into the future; Dr. Thomas Hollon, therapist par excellence, who taught me to value my voice and use my gifts; Dr. Michael Penn, who is contributing much knowledge for the prevention of violence toward women and children worldwide, as well as pulling aside the curtain of darkness that protects the perpetrator; and Daniel Wedemeyer, composer of much of the music in our video about anger, "Louis Timothy, the Giant, Invisible Turtle." I am also grateful to Dr. Marilyn Higgins for her cogent insights, and to therapists

Kathryn Moehling and Sherry Wilson for the offering of their professional dialogue on how to assist the traumatized. Special gratitude to Clifford Moore, the English teacher who helped me develop my love of writing, and to my editor, Ladan Cockshut, who made the editing process painless and guided the book to its truest purpose.

Introduction

When we look at the history of the world, we see that power has consistently been in the hands of rulers and the clergy. There have been autocratic, theocratic, authoritarian, hierarchical, and tyrannical forms of government that have withheld power from the general population. With the arrival of the Revelation of Bahá'u'lláh, we are informed that humankind is at the threshold of spiritual maturity; and therefore, for the first time, the common man and woman are in need of power and in need of having power defined.

What has power to do with assisting the traumatized soul? Many of our ills, both societal and familial, are born of an abuse of power. We see it in the racism that afflicts our country. We see it in the rampant abuse that traumatizes children worldwide, and it is also apparent in the sexism that prevents women from attaining their highest possibilities. Abuse of power and the acquisition of personal power must be addressed if humankind is to be healed of these specific wounds that injure the spirit.

In September of 1997, I attended the Green Lake Bahá'í Conference in Green Lake, Wisconsin. Dr. Michael Penn was one of the speakers on Sunday morning. During his talk he identified spirit injuries as one of the most important discoveries of the twentieth century, and he discussed how they relate to the equality of women and men and, in turn, how the teachings of Bahá'u'lláh can be used to both heal and rectify the imbalance of power between men and women.

Dr. Penn stated,

> The discovery of spirit injuries, an injury in which the physical body, the soma, might show all signs of normality, but the psyche, the spirit, is greatly disturbed, was, to my point of view, one of the most significant discoveries of this century. And now we are aware of a sea of people, male and female, all over the world, suffering spirit injuries for a variety of reasons.
>
> Spirit injuries can be inflicted even with words. The Master makes this very clear. The Master says that if we treat someone with harshness, especially in childhood, we can corrupt their character. These are spirit injuries.
>
> Now there are a lot of people suffering from spirit injuries, and we see the manifestations of these spirit injuries in our communities, in our families, in our own lives. It seems to me that as we address the question of the status of women and equality, one of the areas we can begin to move into is the power of the Cause to heal these spirit injuries and restore the people to spiritual health, to renew them in ways that go far beyond what is presently possible.
>
> I think that the spiritual healing of the women of the world and, indeed, an increasing number of the men of the world, is one of the essential prerequisites for raising the status of women. And I think that globally we have to recognize and accept that these injuries, that these hurts exist and we have to come up with new ways of addressing these problems. And hopefully those who are in psychiatry and psychology will begin to think about how the teachings apply to this question.[1]

With greater and greater frequency, the friends are bringing these spirit injuries to the attention of their Local Spiritual Assemblies, hoping for a measure of guidance and healing. *Assisting the Traumatized Soul* is meant to be a handbook not only for the traumatized themselves but also for the members of the institutions of our Faith, and for the individual seeking to aid those who have suffered oppression.

It can be difficult for a fully mature adult who has been

traumatized to muster up all of the resources and powers in response to the ordeal; imagine how difficult it is to overcome trauma if it is perpetrated before having a fully developed identity, a broad base of rich life experiences, an education that taps inner gifts, and a sense of one's personal power. Because of a grave loss of self-worth, many men and women shrink back from attaining their highest possibilities or expressing the beauty of their individuality. Whatever the type of abuse, be it sexual, physical, mental, emotional, or spiritual, assistance must be seen as a hand extended to an equal, so that the traumatized do not feel as though they are in a "one down" position, for they are keenly aware of the abuse of power.

What does it mean to "assist" a traumatized soul? To answer that question we have to sort through all of the ways we may well-meaningly try to "help" others. Some of us who are quick-thinking may specialize in solving the problems of others through advice-giving, which may be laden with conjecture; others are good at fixing things and may feel confident in offering a "quick fix" to the spiritually injured; still others are accomplished listeners, though they may not know what to do with what they have heard. And some who have strong opinions based on commonly known facts, and are very sure of themselves, may try to "straighten out" the injured person or "convert" them to a more correct way of viewing their problems.[2] The trouble with these commonly accepted methods is that they utilize *our* powers rather than bestowing power or encouraging the development of that power in others. They are also methods that are based upon our own *reality* and may not take into consideration the *reality* of the person who is in desperate need of help.

Our reality is based upon what we assume to be real, our perspective of how things really are, what we are really like, and what the world is like. It also includes our value system: what we think is right or wrong, good or bad, and the values we think are important and believe that everyone else should adopt.[3] Our reality influences how polarized we are in our approach to assisting another; and we cannot afford to be polarized by conflicting theories, principles, psychologies, and philosophies. We need certitude.

Then there is the reality of the traumatized person with whom we are trying to communicate. Their reality is much the same as ours; however, the critical difference is that their reality may not be consciously available to them because they have been traumatized as well as "developmentally disempowered." If we consider only these two points, our power vs. their power, we can readily see that any means we use to assist them must involve the use of "their" power, which we can discover through the process of consultation. "In all things it is necessary to consult," is the advice of Bahá'u'lláh. "The maturity of the gift of understanding is made manifest through consultation."[4] He further states, "No man can attain his true station except through his justice. No power can exist except through unity. No welfare and no well-being can be attained except through consultation."[5]

If we reject their reality, their self-revelation, what else do they have to give us? They would have to limp through life utilizing every psychological defense to hide their reality along with their wounds. It, then, becomes necessary that we listen to them with a discerning ear and without censure, so that we can assist them in having access to their reality, confirming, acknowledging, and reflecting what we hear. We must give up preconceptions about what constitutes immorality, expectations of what they "should" want, need, or do, and predetermined responses based on our reality and what has always worked for us, and remain in an unprogrammed state of inner silence while listening. Then we will be receptive to the reality of the traumatized soul instead of being sealed off from it by "veils." Are these not all the veils that need to be burned away that we might receive knowledge? As the Bahá'í writings state, "Wherefore, if those who have come to the sea of His presence are found to possess none of the limited things of this perishable world, whether it be outer wealth or personal opinions, it mattereth not."[6] And is this not how we may achieve nothingness as a servant of God so that our perception will continue to progress and be refined? For 'Abdu'l-Bahá says, "Once a soul becometh holy in all things, purified, sanctified, the gates of the knowledge of God will open wide before his eyes."[7]

There is yet a third reality, and that is the reality of God that gives our power of perception a foundation of certitude with which to assist the traumatized soul. We know the reality of God through the spiritual principles Bahá'u'lláh revealed. We are told by the Universal House of Justice that it is through these principles that humankind will be induced to act. The power of induction is a very powerful tool for humanity. To induce is to lead. The principles of God, a manifestation of God's truth or "reality," have the power to influence the powers of the traumatized, to lead them, to direct them, to stimulate them, to motivate, galvanize, and actuate them. As the Universal House of Justice, the international governing body of the Bahá'í community, states,

> There are spiritual principles, or what some call human values, by which solutions can be found for every social problem. Any well-intentioned group can in a general sense devise practical solutions to its problems, but good intentions and practical knowledge are usually not enough. The essential merit of a spiritual principle is that it not only represents a perspective which harmonizes with that which is immanent in human nature, but it also induces an attitude, a dynamic, a will, or an aspiration that facilitates the discovery and implementation of practical measures. Leaders of governments and all in authority would be well served in their efforts to solve problems if they would first seek to identify the principles involved and then be guided by them.[8]

Those who want to assist the traumatized soul would also do well to let the spiritual principles of Bahá'u'lláh guide them in their efforts. If we have adopted the reality of God through Bahá'u'lláh's Revelation, we will be less polarized in our thoughts, methods, and behavior and be able to enter the reality of a traumatized person with the consistency and congruence they deserve, without trying to fix, convert, control, or give advice.

We must also help them understand that there is no such thing as moral-free therapy or moral-free listening. All of our listening must be refined and enriched by the *power of discernment* (which is defined on page 63). If we are spiritually discerning, we will be principle-focused, will teach them to be aware of their powers, and will not rest in judgment of their actions. Chapter 4 deals in depth with the God-given *powers,* or abilities, that we all have the opportunity to learn about to develop ourselves spiritually and emotionally.

An important thing to remember is that those who reach out to the traumatized may feel at times that they are taking great risks. Seeking justice and protection for the oppressed will always involve risk. Firm boundaries reduce the risk; and to elect flexible boundaries where appropriate implies a trust that allows for the growth of all concerned. A combination of both is needed from time to time.

One of the things we will have to rid ourselves of is the notion that the traumatized should have "blind faith." This is a simplistic solution that is harmful. It is not the way God works. Look at the miracles and religious myths and stories of the past. One of their purposes is to instill faith in the followers of the religion from which they emanate. Having faith in oneself is perhaps one of the hardest challenges of the healing process. The *power of faith* is defined by 'Abdu'l-Bahá as conscious knowledge (see page 73). If one does not have conscious knowledge, it is very difficult to have faith, especially in oneself. Because the powers of the traumatized are blocked, undeveloped, or forbidden, they do not have conscious knowledge.

When a victim's trauma is acknowledged, their power of faith is increased. Those who have been traumatized need to have their feelings confirmed, their physical pain confirmed, their perceptions confirmed, and their intuition confirmed. That confirmation must be based upon Bahá'í principles.

While the role of the professional in the healing of the traumatized is vital, so too is the role of the community. Local Spiritual Assemblies have to be very discerning about what kind of help they are hoping the spiritually traumatized will seek and find. An excellent choice would be a professional who has successfully integrated the "psychological" and the "spiritual" elements of the human reality. We must also remember that only the writings of the Bahá'í Faith can offer the Divine Elixir that will truly consolidate their wounds and prepare them for the ups and downs of their lifetime journey.[9] And, of course, assisting their power of faith is a spiritual aspect to which the compassionate Bahá'í can attend.

Bahá'u'lláh tells us that we are created noble. If we will but believe in the inherent nobility of those we serve and know that their own sense of their nobility has been fractured and their powers are blocked, we will trust in their goodness when we feel anxious, disappointed, frustrated, and confused by their behavior. This book is not the ultimate voice on what the traumatized can do to heal, nor does it give a complete guide to individuals and communities trying to help the traumatized. What it offers is the experiences of one individual whose life was traumatized but who found a healing balm in the message of Bahá'u'lláh. What it offers is a basic framework for understanding how to assist traumatized souls with dignity, to aid them to find reliable and competent professional help as needed, and to connect them with community resources; and it illustrates with certitude that Bahá'u'lláh's Revelation contains the healing balm of the powers and inner peace of which they were deprived.

Chapter 1

My Own Story

My Own Story

I sit with my two-and-a-half year old grandson on my lap, and waves of memories engulf me. I was as trusting as that once. I was as innocent, too. My grandson has sexual boundaries. Others must protect his sexual boundaries for him until he is old enough to be taught how to protect them himself.

How sad that these are my first thoughts when I am with him, while other parents and grandparents delight in the pure joy of an emerging identity with all of its charm and beauty. It is precisely because we survivors have this sad awareness that the secret of sexual abuse is becoming exposed and sometimes prevented. The secret has always protected the perpetrator of abuse. The perpetrator has always counted on this lack of awareness and lack of boundaries, even believes that this is the way it's supposed to be. For generations, mothers and fathers have cautioned their children to be wary of strangers. Survivors of sexual abuse know that it is the parent, the grandparent, the uncle, the aunt, the friend of the family, the friendly neighbor, who is more likely to be a perpetrator of abuse.

I am fortunate that I am conscious of this. So is my family. Many survivors are not conscious of the need for sexual boundaries, and the chances of their entering into a relationship with someone who would not honor sexual boundaries are very high. Consciousness is good; it doesn't have to be obsessive, just wisely protective. I have taught my adult children protective behavior. It is their responsibility, in turn, to teach their children. To do otherwise would be irresponsible. For generations, ignorance of the problem has been on the side of those who would act out their sickness under the cloak of darkness.

At the age of two I liked to be held. I liked to be touched. I was too young to know the difference between a loving touch and a secret touch. There was no one to protect my innocence, no one to keep me safe until I could protect myself. No one saw the sexual abuse practiced on me by my father when I was my grandson's age. No one in my family recognized the necessity for identity, or physical, spatial, and sexual boundaries in one so young.

Most of the abuse I experienced happened when I was in a drugged state of sleep. My father would come to my bedroom at night, when my mother was asleep and it was safe for him. As the years passed and I grew older, I became more wakeful during these episodes, yet I knew instinctively that I wasn't supposed to be aware of what he was doing. What he was doing was performing the equivalent of oral sex with his fingers.

There was no one to protect me from the abuse, and I was too young to recognize wrong or to gainsay my father, who, as patriarch of an old-fashioned German/Italian family, demanded complete obedience to his authority. I did not know then, of course, that I would spend much of my life seeking ways to repair the damage that my father perpetrated.

One day when I was eight years of age, I was in the living room, one of six happy children, chatting and playing. My father entered the room and sat down in an easy chair. He called me to him. Passively and obediently I went to him. He pulled me up on his lap, placing his hand under my dress, inside my panties. My mother was in the kitchen, unaware. I sat on his lap while he yet again abused me sexually, and I cannot remember feeling any shame. How strange it seems to me now, and how sad.

Then one day, the hand of God intervened. My oldest sister told my mother what was happening. My mother lay awake that night, pretending she was asleep. When my father got out of bed and stealthily approached my bedroom, she sat up and asked him what he was doing. He told her he was checking on the children. She confronted him with the accusation my sister had made. He admitted his wrongdoing. She told him that from then on she would check on the children.

In retrospect, I can see that my mother was faced with a very difficult situation. I know now that she instinctively did her best to protect her children's future. I credit her courage, tenacity, and willingness to suffer to keep the family together as among the sources of my healing. Because she kept the family together through all of its future tragedies, I was eventually able to trace patterns of abuse through three generations and make some sense of our suffering.

I also credit my father for his honesty when my mother questioned him about the accusation his oldest daughter had made. For without that admission of guilt, my perception that the abuse had actually happened, which was also vitally necessary for my healing, would have been severely discounted. Other survivors of sexual abuse are not as fortunate, and doubt is cast on them by themselves and others, which hinders their recovery.

Abuse: A Family Inheritance

As I later learned, my father had been physically, if not sexually, abused as a child by my grandfather. An alcoholic who may even have been psychotic, my grandfather seemed to hate my father, beating him regularly and using him almost as a slave to the rest of the family. Though all of my father's siblings were abused, my father was the most abused child.

My grandfather is known to have committed bestiality, and I believe he may have perpetrated a very aggressive type of sexual abuse on his children as well. My father's sister has told me that when my father was about ten years old, she saw him run out of the barn completely naked, crying so hard that his eyes were swollen shut. I have also been told that when he was fifteen years old, the police locked him up in the local jail to protect him from my grandfather, who was chasing him with an ax. I am also told that my grandfather beat my father regularly with a bullwhip.

My father was artistic, but he hid this side of himself and destroyed his sketches because he feared the ridicule and abuse of others. In his family, daring to express his thoughts and dreams meant punishment and judgment because it was their habit to cruelly ridicule and belittle one another. There was no chance for his talent, or even for his mental faculties, to develop fully; he had been forced to quit school in the eighth grade to work and help support the family. For the rest of his life, he was frustrated by his inability to read well enough even to understand newspaper articles.

Following in my grandfather's footsteps, my father ran his home in an extremely authoritarian manner, requiring complete obedience from his children. Like his father, he was brutally abusive to his children. He would not allow any of us to speak without intimidating or ridiculing us; we children were not allowed to speak while eating, working, or preparing for bed. We had to whisper to each other, and if we were heard whispering in bed, we were berated or beaten.

My father had a perverse sense of humor and seemed to be obsessed with sex. He falsely accused all of his daughters of "whoring around" when we were teenagers. The truth was, we were extremely unsophisticated children who were sheltered socially by his fears. I am assuming that his guilty conscience and his own obsession about sex drove him to disallow us participation in extracurricular activities in school, so that he could keep a watchful eye on us.

The only respite we had from him was when he was at work, when we were sent to the movies once a week on Saturday, and when we were at school or church. I learned never to stay at home when I could get away to church, and I never invited anyone to my home. Even today I find myself feeling sad and anxious if I stay in my house for too many hours in one day. At 54 years of age, I am only just now beginning to feel comfortable when people visit me in my home. A few years back I invited my support group to my home for a slumber party and had to ask a friend to take charge while I went to bed for two hours.

Keeping the Secret

Though today I have told my story many times over, the majority of my childhood was governed by "the secret." In 1986, at the age of 45, I was to write in my journal the following entry that describes the plight of most survivors of sexual abuse:

Please don't look too closely at me. You might see my secret.
Please don't talk to me. I might accidentally tell you my
secret. No, I don't want to be friends. Friends tell secrets.
No, I don't want that promotion. I'm too occupied with my
secret. And I can't express an opinion either. You might
guess my secret. No, I'm not going to invite you to my
home. We have a houseful of secrets! What's the sense of
sharing feelings? People with secrets avoid them. And no, I
can't tell you what my secret is. It's so secret, I may not be
fully conscious of it.

This is the universal power of the secret. To protect their secrets,
survivors withdraw into themselves, always keeping others at a
distance. I also decided to protect my family at all costs, to be
"perfect," never to talk to anyone about my abuse for fear of
being locked up, not to ask questions out of fear of being beaten,
to be obedient at all times, to be passive and compliant, and
never to express anger about anything.

   "Behave, or we'll lock you in the basement!" "Be good, or
we'll put you in reform school!" "Be loyal to the family at all
costs, or all of your brothers and sisters will be put in the
children's home or foster homes!" What kind of fear and
desperation drove my parents to give their children such messages? That is the power of the secret. My parents kept the secret.
Aunts and uncles kept the secret. Grandparents kept the secret.
Children kept the secret.

   It is not surprising that people don't want to reveal the
depravity in their families. It is not pretty. It is not a topic for
polite company. But, apart from the tiresome sensationalism
created by the topic of incest as it is exploited on daytime
television talk shows, one of the priceless benefits of revealing
the secret is that it enables those who have been traumatized to
begin the process of healing.

An Emotional Roller Coaster

Two things occurred to make me feel that I was to blame for
what had happened: the silence surrounding the issue and the
fact that I was my father's "favorite child." Part of my socializa-
tion process, through my teenage years, took place in a Baptist

church in Rockford, Illinois. There I learned about the doctrine of original sin while watching a film depicting people screaming and burning in hell. This, to me, at the tender age of ten in 1951, confirmed that I was to blame for what had happened to me. I knew then that I had participated in something evil, yet I also realized that it was implicitly approved by my father, the most important authority figure in my life at that time. Thus began the conflict of values that I was to act out in self-destructive ways for the next forty-five years, a moral conflict that was to torment me emotionally without my being able to identify it intellectually or verbally.

Many times I had the feeling I was sliding uncontrollably into a chasm of terror. The emotional goal for children and teenagers is stability. This is assisted by parents who guide the child into sharing feelings verbally. When the long-unconscious side of me began to surface during my teenage years, I had no one to help me make sense of the emotional roller coaster I was experiencing. I was not promiscuous as a teenager, but my repressed thoughts and sexual fantasies were becoming more and more threatening. I would act out my unconscious moral conflicts in actions rather than words—in seductive ways, sometimes subtle, sometimes blatant.

When I was fourteen years old, I was attracted to a married man in our neighborhood. I pretended to visit his wife, but would tease him seductively and innocently, until one day he violently pushed me against the wall, pressing his full body against mine. I felt great shame. I didn't think that was what I wanted. Was this just my coming of age as a woman? I don't think so. What was the real reason I visited the Army, Navy, and Air Force enlistment offices on a regular weekly basis from age fifteen through seventeen? Was this just raging hormones? I don't think so. Team raging hormones with parental authority covertly condoning sex by encouraging sexual feelings in a small child, and thereby making it the unconscious focus of the life of a child, and I think we can see it in a truer light.

One day I sat on a youth's lap in church. On another occasion my home economics teacher came into the classroom and found me sitting on a young man's lap. She scolded me and sent me to the office. Clearly this was inappropriate behavior, but it is certainly understandable for someone who had been sexually abused on her father's lap. But no one—not even I—made that connection at the time. It never occurred to me that I was acting out sexually. I would not even learn that term until I was in my forties. I had all this unconscious sexual power that was approved by my father, yet not approved. It was as if I was drawn to anything with even a vapor of seduction, like the lifting of an eyebrow on the face of a movie star, and instantly I would add it to my unconscious collection of subtle seductive tricks.

As a result of such incidents, I became morally hypervigilant as a young adult. I thought I needed to protect myself from an external threat, but the real threat was the unknown, unconscious side of me that was becoming more and more active. The excessive sexual content of my thoughts was causing me increasing terror.

I was making a conscious effort to live what I perceived to be a moral life, while unconsciously my behavior was contradicting that morality. There were times when I became aware of this unconscious behavior. I was dumbfounded and ashamed of the inconsistencies and would punish myself for the transgressions. I became extremely controlling, always hyper alert, yet eventually I would lapse again into unconscious behavior that betrayed what I was trying so desperately to hide.

In August of 1959, I was awarded a music scholarship from my Baptist Church to attend the Baptist Bible College in Denver, Colorado. This is where I met my first husband on a blind date, January 8, 1960. We saw each other every day for two weeks. I violated the school rules by going to the theatre to see the movie *Porgy and Bess*. The Dean of the school sent me home in shame at the end of January because they thought I was sleeping with the young man I was seeing. They were wrong. The young man asked me to marry him before I left Denver. I said "yes," and it was decided that I would return home and wait until he sent for me. I worked for a finance company for a month, earning enough money to take the bus to Kansas City, Missouri, where his mother lived at the time.

"If you run away to marry him, I'll follow you, and I'll find you. I'll tell him you have nigger blood in you so he won't want to marry you. So no one will want to marry you, you whore!" my father had said. With the assistance of my mother, I called the police, had them escort me to the bus station, and left Rockford in total fear, in total depression. My mother met me at the station to say good-bye to me. She was always there to protect her children from their father.

I had left college in shame with no one to advocate for me; I had left home in shame with the label "whore" ringing in my ears; and I had left my innocent, defenseless brothers and sisters in an extremely violent environment with no hope of safety, love, or protection from a raging father. Sitting behind the bus driver in the dark, my shame increased as I allowed him to run his hand up and down my leg. How could I do that when I professed to love the man I was going to meet in Kansas City? I took a taxi to my future mother-in-law's home, aware that I was in danger of acting out with the driver. I stayed in Kansas City until my future husband had transferred to Texas. His mother bought me a wedding dress before I left to join him in Fort Worth in March of 1960.

I was terrified that my father had followed me to Texas. I looked over my shoulder at all times, watching for his green pickup truck. Every time I saw a green truck, I had a rush of adrenalin and picked up my pace to duck inside a store. I was that terrified.

We were married on April 16, 1960. I got pregnant the following month. I was nauseated for a full 5½ months and lost twenty pounds. I'm not surprised that my daughter was such a tiny baby when she was born. It's a wonder she got any nourishment, I was so sick.

We didn't have enough money for food when I was pregnant. My husband was an Airman Third Class in the Air Force and on that salary we had barely enough money to eat more than soup. What preserved my baby's development in the womb was the fact that I was on vitamins for my pregnancy. I was starving and nauseous at the same time. My husband didn't understand that I wasn't getting enough to eat, and I didn't know how to tell him. I couldn't ask him for money because I didn't know how. It was my perception that I wasn't allowed to ask for money, not from my parents, not from my husband. So I slept through my nine months of pregnancy. My husband didn't know what behavior to expect of a pregnant woman or the needs that I would have, but he really did his best to care for us on what little knowledge he had. He also didn't recognize that my sleeping an inordinate amount of time was a symptom of deep depression, a desire to escape, as well as being caused by the changes in my body due to the pregnancy.

My daughter was born at Carswell Air Force Base Hospital in Fort Worth, Texas, on February 8, 1961. I was nineteen years old. I remember being sad and very disturbed in the hospital because my mother couldn't come. I remember crying. The nurses said that I was too emotionally upset for my milk "to come down." I kept trying to nurse; but my baby wasn't getting anything. She kept losing weight. She weighed 5 pounds, 4 ounces at birth and after three days weighed 4 pounds, 10 ounces. The nurses then took matters into their own hands and put her on a bottle. The hospital policy stated that babies under five pounds could not leave the hospital. They sent me home. They kept my baby for seven days. I was very disturbed because they wouldn't let me have her.

When my daughter did come home, she was not a responsive baby. She did not smile throughout her infancy. I was inept. My husband had to fix the formula for me. I didn't know how to do it; but he did. At that time in my life, I just let people move me around; things just happened. I didn't make them happen. Things worked because everyone told me what to do. My husband always knew what to do, and I trusted that. Life was very simple for me because I didn't make any choices.

I remember being proud of my baby and wanting to be a good mother, but I was always aware that I needed to have someone there with me. I needed someone to watch me so I would be good, so I would be sure to do things right. It was as though I couldn't be good unless there was someone there to be good in front of. This thought was continually part of my consciousness. I didn't know the right way to act.

One of the things that helped me to become more conscious was the positive attention I received from my husband's grandparents, our daughter's great-grandparents. We brought our baby to visit their farm in Durant, Oklahoma, and received many gifts.

Some months later we returned to Durant, and Grandma Stone commented on the baby's lack of weight gain. At this point I was beginning to feel more inept. The depression of having left my sisters and brothers in danger was ever present in my mind. I remember that I couldn't always remember to feed my baby and take care of her needs. She developed a diaper rash of which I was very ashamed. It developed into large, open, painful sores all over her bottom. I tried everything, powder, lotion, creams. However, I left her in her wet diapers too long, for hours sometimes. I couldn't remember to change her. I would go back to sleep. The ammonia in her diapers was fierce and overpowering. The sores were very painful, but she was stoic and did not cry about them. She tried to move away to keep her diaper from touching them, but she did not cry. Grandma Stone must have been very shocked. The open sores finally healed when she was potty trained, but there were scars on her bottom. I was so ashamed. I had no one with whom to share my shame, my thoughts, or my worries.

I couldn't remember to feed her. I wanted to sleep, and she would cry. I would get up and feed her a cracker to quiet her, then I would go back to bed. But I didn't feed her. I think I couldn't remember to feed her because no one was present to watch. Then, one day, I believe God intervened. I had picked up a magazine and begun reading a story about a woman who was an alcoholic. She was so drunk that when her baby in the playpen cried, she threw her a cracker to quiet her. If she was drunk all day, the baby was fed crackers all day. It was a sobering story for me. I began to try harder.

In my shame and eagerness to correct my ways, I tried to introduce new foods to my baby, and she kept gagging on them. I didn't know that new foods should be introduced slowly. I was discouraged. She fought me. This was the beginning of my forcing her. I had to force her with food, medicine, ear drops. I equated forcing her with being the best mother I could be.

I was married to my first husband for 12 years and we had three wonderful children. My husband and my children suffered from the fact that we did not know how the sexual abuse perpetrated against me during childhood had affected our family. I never revealed my secret to him. I thought that no man would have wanted me as his wife had he known. I was never unfaithful to him in the sense that violation of marriage vows would imply; but I could never reconcile my unfaithful thoughts or character. I believed I was damned because of my secret character. I believed that it was rooted in the doctrine of original sin. And with that kind of belief system, how could I find any answers? The answers came in an unexpected way in 1964.

OKINAWA!

We were transferred from Fort Worth to Okinawa, Japan. My husband left for Okinawa first after moving myself and our children to Rockford, thinking that it would be better if we were near family until we joined him. I developed a mysterious nervous tic upon moving back into my parents' house. We lived there from June through October, at which time we flew to Okinawa, where my nervous tic mysteriously disappeared. Years later I connected the appearance of the tic with my fear of entering my father's presence.

Two major things happened to me on Okinawa. First, I was exposed to a multitude of religious beliefs which led me to question Christianity as it had been taught to me. If the Lutherans, the Presbyterians, the Catholics, the Methodists, and the members of other denominations who had befriended me at the base chapel (which held rotating services for all) were so incredibly beautiful and dedicated to Christ, how could they all be going to hell, as the Baptists had taught me? It blew me away!

I visited Buddhist and Shinto temples; I explored the island. The Okinawan people weren't heathen, as the Baptists had forewarned me. I was touched by their beauty and their generosity to me. My mind exploded. It was a moment of truth that changed me forever. I didn't know it then, but on my return to the States I would become a "seeker," thirsting for a spiritual atmosphere that would be inclusive rather than exclusive.

The second thing that changed my life was a decision to perform on stage. My husband observed that I was "doing better" when I was performing. I believe that "doing better" meant having a creative outlet that relieved my sadness and anxiety. With this creative outlet came more freedom; but because of my dark side, I couldn't handle that much freedom.

On Okinawa, I began attracting the kind of men who could really hurt me. They were like me, in grave need of spiritual guidance. This was during the Vietnam War in the mid-1960s, when people were testing the limits of conventional morality. No longer sheltered, I entered into superficial relationships that were extremely risky. The risk carried a thrill, but it also carried a consequence. I was headed for a real downhill slide if I didn't pull back, and I was finally conscious of it, though I didn't know what to do. I was growing more calculating and developing a "hardness of heart" with each risk I took. With each risk there came a growing fear, which I believe was connected to the development of my power of discernment.[1] But I was still a little girl seeking the power of my father's attention, the only power I really wanted.

First Encounter with the Faith

When my husband's tour of duty ended in 1967, we returned to the States, settling in the Dallas area. We began to search for a new church, because we could not return to a traditional Christian worship. We sampled theosophy, Rosicrucianism, and others. My husband was offered a job in Rockford, and we returned in January of 1968, still searching for a religion that was compatible with our beliefs. We began attending both Jewish and Unitarian services.

We learned of the Bahá'í Faith in 1969 through a newspaper announcement regarding an upcoming informational meeting. I was apprehensive as my husband and I approached the door to the home of the Bahá'í couple who introduced us to the Faith, but my fears were swept away by the warmth and love inside. And when I learned about the teachings of Bahá'u'lláh I knew that this was the inclusive religion I had been looking for.

Looking for ways to teach the Faith, I began to perform as an entertainer again. Once again, the downhill slide began. I was out of control! My highs were extremely high, my lows were extremely low. I began to pull further away from my husband.

This type of sickness, this type of immorality cannot be wished or prayed away. It's not a matter of willpower. I imagine we all come to the Bahá'í Faith with our own set of problems. We can't foresee how the Faith is going to change our lives. We cannot conceive yet of the real power to heal that is embedded in the Bahá'í writings or the real interest that Bahá'u'lláh devotes to us as individuals. I believe it was through God's grace and bounty that I recognized Bahá'u'lláh. I know I was on a self-destructive path, wandering and stumbling around blindly from one dangerous situation to another, even amid God's bounty and grace. The Bahá'í Faith seemed like a point of light on that path. I made friends as a new Bahá'í. I taught the Faith to others. For two years I studied the Faith, and I was moved by the spiritual truths I discovered, especially the principle of individual investigation of truth. This principle implies the right to ask questions, which at that time was beyond my ability.

And then, in the short four-month period, from October 1971 to January 1972, I got a divorce; I put my aged, loyal dog to sleep; and my father, my abuser, died of lung cancer at 53 years of age. Considering my emotional instability at the time, even one of these events could have caused me to lose my balance. I dearly loved my dog, I took care of my father during the last weeks of his life, and my husband was probably the best friend I had ever had in my life.

I did not cry. I did not feel anything. I went into a trancelike state during which I heard voices. The voices said, "Give everything away." I asked, "Where should I start?" The reply was, "Start with the kitchen table." I said, "Of course, none of it is mine anyway!"

Slowly, methodically, one trip at a time, I loaded up the trunk and backseat of my 1968 black Dodge Dart. I gave everything away—beds, stereos, bookshelves, knock-down furniture, pots, pans, and blankets—to Bahá'ís, neighbors, hippies, and strangers. It was a Herculean effort for one very weak woman. However, in what I later came to recognize as a manic state, I was capable of almost anything.

When I finished, I went across the street to a neighbor. She took me into her arms and rocked me and crooned to me. It was a quiet moment of rest after a very busy day. But it was also the nurturing of the child with stunted emotional growth within me who could neither look to the future nor understand the consequences of what she had done or the reasons behind it. There was no thought of the future. Just a quiet trust.

My children slept at my neighbor's home that night. I went back to my empty house and lay down on the carpet in my bedroom. I went into a trance again, and in my trance the voice said, "The police are going to come and get you now." The doorbell rang, and I went downstairs to open the door. The police were there, so I let them in. I had no fear, I felt no need or desire to resist. They brought me to a mental health facility.

When I awoke the next day, I was in terror! My deepest fear had come to pass: I was locked up! I was no longer in a trance. This was a harsh reality! My Local Spiritual Assembly had reported my bizarre behavior. For seven days I pretended to be as normal as possible and did my best to explain my behavior. I refused medication. I refused to admit that there was anything wrong with me.

A female therapist, a Muslim, interviewed me. She appeared to be extremely angry with me because of what I was putting my children through by giving away everything that belonged to them. She asked me what was my religion. I told her I was a Bahá'í. She asked me what frightened me. I told her that I was afraid people were trying to turn me into a prostitute. To my surprise, she asked why I didn't want to be a prostitute. I replied that it wouldn't be good for my children. She sneered at me and cruelly asked why I didn't give my children away and go do what I really wanted to do. I was stunned. Adrenalin—and a wave of shame and panic—shot through me. I couldn't think. I couldn't even speak up for myself. I had no concept that she, the "authority," should be reported. I believe her negative response to me was because of her religious prejudice. I'm sure she was concerned about my children but it also appeared that she believed my religious beliefs were harmful to my children and that she had a wrathful concept of God.

I decided to refuse all help from that moment on, because the therapist had taken my deepest fear and twisted it. I was afraid that if I took any medicine I would lose control and they would be able to turn me into a prostitute or I wouldn't be able to defend myself. I refused to drink out of the drinking fountain, thinking they had put medicine in it. Terror and anxiety pushed me to roam the halls reciting the Lord's Prayer nonstop. I was terrified that someone would attack me while I was sleeping. I forced myself to remain awake as long as I could. After brief periods of sleep I would awake to panic and wave after wave of adrenalin.

After seven days I was released from the mental health facility. They had tried to make me admit to being suicidal. Because I had no conscious thoughts of suicide, I could not admit to it. That had been the basis for the Local Spiritual Assembly's signing me into the facility. I can't blame the Local Spiritual Assembly today, but I was very angry with them at the time. As a result of a variety of conflicting emotions, I formally withdrew from the Faith, although it would not leave my heart and mind. I loved the Faith so much, but the caring and responsible aspect of my character could not in good conscience remain a Bahá'í because I knew I was unable to remain celibate and did not want to hurt the teaching efforts of others.

The Unconscious Self Revealed

It was to be ten years before I returned to the Faith. During those ten years I ostracized myself from the rest of the world because I felt I had to protect people from my depravity. During this self-imposed banishment from society, I prayed that Bahá'u'lláh would heal me. I prayed for celibacy, I prayed for chastity of mind, I prayed that if there were books that could help me heal, I would be able to find them. I read everything in sight on healing, psychology, and religion. Unconsciously, I was refusing to face my situation, denying the emotional impact of my problems. I was in an unaware, trance-like condition known to psychologists as "dissociation," though I was not to learn the term for several years. At the time, I would not turn to a psychologist; I didn't trust them. I was developing my ability to conduct an independent search for truth. This required that I learn to talk, to ask questions, and to be aware.

To heal, it was vital that the dark side of me become fully

conscious and accountable. However, that process would be a trauma in its own right because I would have to meet the sexually obsessed person who was a product of six dark years of sexual abuse. Developmentally, this darker side of me was less than eight years old, probably much younger. She was raw, she would not take "no" for an answer. She was repulsive, vulgar, full of rage, perverted, depraved, and only minimally verbal. She had delusions of grandeur and power, and she was uncontrollable. She had no fear of God, she was shameless, and she was me.

At the age of thirty, in the summer of 1971, I caught a glimpse of her unexpectedly when I was telling a male acquaintance, a musician, about a man with whom I thought I was in love. We were sitting in his car after we had performed at a local night spot. He asked, "How do you know you love him?" I said in a strange, tiny voice that sounded like a very little girl, "I can't tell you, but I can show you." He looked at me intently for a moment, then pulled back and said, "My God! Your lips are swollen and you look like an animal!" Who was this strange person who created such revulsion in others and shame in me? Praise God, I was finally conscious of her presence!

I did not know that I was going to recognize the presence of this other person within myself or this facet of my fragmented identity. I could not understand it. But a quotation from Bahá'u'lláh now comes to mind: "Liberty causeth man to overstep the bounds of propriety, and to infringe on the dignity of his station. It debaseth him to the level of extreme depravity and wickedness."[2] The darker side of me did not know that there were bounds of propriety. How could she? She had been created in the dark by someone who had taken liberty with God's creation and had perverted it.

Much later I was to learn through therapy that even this display of swollen lips that so shocked and disgusted my acquaintance was the expression of a normal sexuality. Perhaps my acquaintance interpreted it as abnormal, and perhaps the undeveloped part of me was using it in an innocent way. The adult woman that I was at the time was demonstrating how sexual stimulation could cause a rush of blood to any part of the body that is so stimulated either physically or through fantasy. In any case, the controlling side of me, whom I call my "internal eunuch" because she found any sexual activity abhorrent, named that other part of myself a "sexualized creature." My whole and gentler true self calls it the "sexualized child," who, because of her age and because of the interruption of her normal development, could not be expected to control her sexuality. The truth is that children and even babies have sexual organs and express innocent sexuality. It is normal, healthy, and documented. But when an adult uses those normal responses from a child to satisfy their own sexual needs, that child's innocent sexuality becomes perverted. This phenomenon explains why children who are sexually abused usually blame themselves for the abuse. The perversion of their sexuality appears to be proof of guilt, yet nothing could be further from the truth.

Shoghi Effendi, the Guardian of the Bahá'í Faith, says that even as children, we are inclined toward evil. "The child when born is far from being perfect. It is not only helpless but actually imperfect, and even is naturally inclined toward evil."[3] Because it is a characteristic of the soul to mirror what is put in front of it, when evil is mirrored to us in early childhood, we will mirror it back because we have not yet developed the ability to choose, nor can we properly conceptualize obedience to the laws of God.

The Bahá'í concept of evil is more of a continuum that ranges from imperfection and lack of education at one end of the scale, to perfection and education at the other end of the scale— perfection being something to strive for, but something we will never reach. This continuum has many variables in that, though we all have the power to recognize God, we each have different capacities or inherent knowledge. Also, we may have been conditioned (acquired knowledge) before we received a spiritual education. So no two of us can be judged by a single scale of perfection and imperfection. My conditioning was in direct conflict with the Revelation of Bahá'u'lláh, and certainly placed me in the position of being viewed as evil in the traditional Christian understanding of the concept. However, as the following quotation reveals, the laws of God must be taught to children to enable them to have strong boundaries and a fear of God which motivates them to strive toward moral behavior.

Concerning the education of children, Bahá'u'lláh has said,

> That which is of paramount importance for the children,
> that which must precede all else, is to teach them the
> oneness of God and the laws of God. For lacking this, the
> fear of God cannot be inculcated, and lacking the fear of
> God an infinity of odious and abominable actions will
> spring up and sentiments will be uttered that transgress all
> bounds . . .[4]

If I had had my present language and knowledge when I became
conscious of a dark facet of my identity, my question would have
been, "Can the darker side of me be reformed through learning
the laws of God?" Was the developmentally delayed part of
myself capable of being taught and retaining her lessons, or was
her sexually obsessed character, including her thoughts, behavior, and motivations, permanently perverted? Apparently, she
was educable, or I would not have had the ensuing lessons and
experiences that I am about to relate.

In late 1972 I started attending a nonsectarian church. I wrote
a story titled *Skylark, the Bird Who Learned to Fly,* which was about
a bird who was abused in the nest. He decided that he wasn't
supposed to fly. He was taught by a bird named Dovie that he
could fly if he took responsibility for his life. Enlisting the help of
the children in the church, I created puppets, and the play was
produced for a Sunday morning presentation in the spring of
1973. I was exhilarated when my Skylark puppet, aided by a tiny
screw at the top of his head and a fishing pole at the side of the
church, flew into the audience at the end, yelling, "I can fly! I can
fly! I can flyyyyyyyyyyy!"

With the success of my puppet show, I felt a little more equal
with others. Feeling equal was very important to me. I decided to
tell the minister of the church what I was going through,
thinking that it was a preferable alternative to entering into
therapy. It was a mistake. During counseling, the minister tried
to seduce me. Then he gave me a book entitled *Open Marriage* to
read. I knew instantly that it was not what I wanted or needed. I
left his home in an anxiety attack. I left the church, too. What

was my participation in his attempt at seduction? I didn't know if it was my fault, but I couldn't be sure! All I knew was that I didn't feel safe, so I moved on. (Twenty years later the minister was ousted from the church because of his sexual behavior with many of the women of his congregation.)

I would alternately do something very inappropriate in clothing that was seductive, become horror-stricken, and then step into my other, more modest wardrobe, keeping everyone at arm's length. But I did not connect any of this with the sexual abuse that had occurred early in my childhood.

I wanted very much to sing professionally and had sung in nightclubs and churches off and on from an early age. Singing gave my soul release, but it was also a threatening activity for my internal eunuch, who linked it with evil and sexuality because I felt more like a sexualized person than a vocalist who was dedicated to her craft. The following is a painful excerpt from my journal, illustrating the distorted thoughts that originated from a conflict between the person I wanted to be, the internal eunuch who ruthlessly denied any and all sexuality, and the sexualized child who inhabited the deepest chasm of my mind:

> Don't sing! Singing attracts people to me. To sing would be the greatest expression of my sexuality. I am not sexual. I do not have sexual needs. Other people do but I don't. I want nothing to do with sex. Sex is evil. All of these problems I'm having, the break-up of my marriage, my acting out, everything is happening because I wanted to sing professionally. I feel threatened when I sing because I feel sexual and I make people think sexual thoughts. I feel like I'm going to lose control. What are these strange feelings in my abdomen? I don't want these feelings. They scare me! If I sing, I will become promiscuous. People will find out that I am evil!

This thought process was repeated whenever the sexualized child would emerge—whenever I fantasized about sex or even thought of acting out sexually. I could neither say "no" nor move away if someone made inappropriate sexual advances toward me. I felt paralyzed. At thirty-two years of age, I still had no ability to govern my own actions, to recognize right and wrong, to make my own choices, and to take personal responsibility for my life.

Being confronted with the need to make a decision would set off an anxiety attack. Choice terrified me, whether it was an important decision or unimportant. A thing as simple as the desire to go to the grocery store was suspect. I did not know who was making the choices. I was in danger with every choice that the sexualized child, my internal eunuch, or all three of us made.

I truly did not know myself, and I did not want to know this sexually obsessed child. But I have come to accept her. I coexist with her now because she and I are accountable to Bahá'u'lláh. I protect her, and I protect myself from her. She still makes my life miserable from time to time, but it is a conscious misery. I am not fighting an unknowable apparition. I am wrestling with the keeper of the memories.

Here's an example of some of the misery she caused me before I befriended her. At one point about a year after my divorce, I convinced myself that the man who lived across the street from me was going to break down my door and rape me. In a panic, I feverishly sewed myself into my sleeping bag. My reasoning was that I could yell for my children to help me before my neighbor could break through the stitching on the bag. The next morning, my irrational state was replaced by embarrassment when my nine-year-old son came into the room and saw me, chin pressed down upon my chest, trying to chew my way out of the sleeping bag. After I had sewn the bag up to my neck, I had put my arms down to my sides inside the bag and could not get them back up the next morning.

My son began, "Mom, why did you—?" Then, embarrassed for me, he shook his head and left me to my task. I am alternately amused and saddened when I remember this incident. Telling the story at workshops among other survivors of sexual abuse is an occasion for tremendous discharge of nervous energy through hysterical laughter. It is comforting to know that others have been this frightened and irrational, too. I'm glad I have gained some perspective that allows me to laugh at myself. To this day I can't determine whether I was trying to keep myself in or him out.

The morally hypervigilant internal eunuch also caused me difficulties. One day while working, I thought, "I'll start singing with a band again. I'll call a musician. I'll make an appointment. That would be wonderful. It would be fun."

I looked up the name and phone number of a musician, called him, and there was no answer. I put the phone in its cradle again and began to type. The internal eunuch went to work. "What have you done? What are you planning? They're going to turn you into a prostitute. You're going to lose your children and your job!" She droned on and on with catastrophe after catastrophe until I ran to the bathroom, locked the door, and began beating myself with my fists all over my body. I slapped my face, I pinched and twisted my skin, and I pummeled myself. At the end of the day I had bruises.

This was a very important lesson for me. God knew my weakness. "None can escape the snares He setteth, and no soul can find release except through submission to His will."[5] I believe He sometimes set the snare, or tested me, with another person, whom He knew intimately, who had the same weakness, so that both of us would experience an expansion of consciousness, or spiritual growth. That is His mercy. I experienced the pain of my choices and the inconvenience of their consequences (anxiety attacks) again and again until I achieved expansion of consciousness, or until I could not bear the pain and shame or inconvenience anymore. I made the choice to align my thoughts and behavior with the teachings of Bahá'u'lláh. This was the healing power of obedience to God.

'Abdu'l-Bahá uses the term "expansion of consciousness." This phrase can prove very helpful to those who dissociate. My consciousness had to expand to envelop the unconscious motivations of the sexualized child. If I continued to escape into a trance, I would be shutting down my mind when I could be using it to solve my problems. This means that dissociation, a defense mechanism that was useful to me when I needed to be protected from the reality of the abuse, was now undermining my efforts to improve my moral choices and behavior.

> There are certain pillars which have been established as
> the unshakable supports of the Faith of God. The mightiest
> of these is learning and the use of the mind, the expansion of
> consciousness, and insight into the realities of the universe
> and the hidden mysteries of Almighty God.[6]

I had to trust that God was providing lessons to expand my
consciousness because He thought I was capable of understanding and because He wanted to use me in a greater capacity.
Indeed, He leads us to trust during tribulation with the following
verse: "I know of a certainty, by virtue of My love for Thee, that
Thou wilt never cause tribulations to befall any soul unless Thou
desirest to exalt his station in Thy Celestial Paradise."[7] The
expansion of consciousness led me to new perceptions. New
perceptions led to new choices. The increasing stability of my
chaste volition became the foundation for a greater expansion of
consciousness.

Often our tests lie within us. Our life experience engages
them. They are embedded in our nobility, or the angelic side of
us. Our inner vision is a witness to our behavior. The script of
our unconscious beliefs about what constitutes appropriate or
inappropriate behavior is our test. Life tests our nobility with
opportunities for chastity and justice in community with others.
Our beliefs emerge for us to witness in our actions. It is then that
we compare our beliefs to God's Word. This is why we are called
to bring ourselves to account each day by scrutinizing our
actions:

> O SON OF BEING!
> Bring thyself to account each day ere thou art summoned to
> a reckoning; for death, unheralded, shall come upon thee
> and thou shalt be called to give account for thy deeds.[8]

Exposure to the Word of God shows us how our beliefs are
distorted and permits the healthy development of the faculty of
shame as well as the fear of God. Such changes lead to new
perceptions and new choices that reflect accountability and lead
to spiritual transformation.

Eventually I began to understand that obedience leads to

psychological stability, and, conversely, that disobedience leads to instability. Shoghi Effendi confirms this in a letter written on his behalf to an individual believer:

> Physical healing cannot be complete and lasting unless it is reinforced by spiritual healing. And this last one can be best obtained through obedience to the laws and commandments of God as revealed to us through His Manifestations.[9]

I also realized that my accountability to Bahá'u'lláh must lead to setting boundaries for the sexualized child, though I could not articulate that concept at the time; the internal eunuch dealt with her. I now describe this process as setting internal boundaries for the sexualized child and setting external boundaries for myself and limits for others.

My capacity for separating my perception, reflection, memory, discernment, and volition from that of others was developing. Having a clear sense of self was very difficult for me, but I was beginning to "see" myself. Some clear boundaries began to be delineated in my consciousness, indicating that I was beginning to accept the fact that I had some limitations.

Two amazing things happened to me when I recognized that I had boundaries. I found a job! I was very shaky on the job for the first two months of 1974. I was terrified that the real reason I got the job was because the "devil" had a plan to turn me into a prostitute. I thought He was going to do it with the help of my employer. Because of severe depression with suicidal thoughts, I asked for help at a mental health clinic. I was diagnosed as having clinical depression and was put on a medication that helped me to keep my job, though I continued to "look over my shoulder" for three years for signs that my employer and his staff were going to force me to become a prostitute.

The next facet of myself that I was to discover and direct was my emotions. In 1975, when my children were 14, 12, and 11 years old, I enrolled in a parenting class at the YMCA because I felt I was a failure as a parent. In the absence of my former husband, I now raged at my oldest child. But the most astonishing thing occurred. One entire two-hour class session was devoted to teaching us about feelings. I clearly realized that I knew nothing about feelings. I recognized that I had been trying to prevent my children from feeling anger or sadness about my divorcing their father. After the class, I went home and opened my manuscript, *Skylark, the Bird Who Learned to Fly*. I examined the pages, searching for words that expressed feelings. There were none. I had described conditions, actions, events, people, plot, thoughts, and characters, but there was no description of emotion; no feeling words had been used for Skylark to explain his emotional condition after years of abuse.

Before making this discovery, I would take out the manuscript every six months or so just to look at it and wonder what to do with it. But now I had something to reflect on deeply. I went to work rewriting the Skylark manuscript. This was great intellectual work for me; but I still could not feel my own emotions. However, this was a beginning; I was able to identify and match feelings to situations on paper and orally. Yet except for my rage and shame which should have been examined in the context of the sexual abuse and directed at my father, I remained emotionally numb.

I painted ninety-seven watercolor illustrations for the Skylark story, recorded the narrative on audio tape, and turned it into a slide show. I began presenting programs for parents, nursing homes, schools, churches, and others. This boosted my self-esteem and feeling of equality as I timidly reentered society. As I taught others, I began to learn more, to tell more of my own story, though guardedly, and to internalize the concept of responsibility for oneself. This was quite an achievement, after horrendous fear had driven me to the brink of destroying the work at least eight times over a period of six years. I thought this truth would destroy my family. I was terrified of my creativity; it led me to truth. The subconscious fear that I had was this: If I tell the truth about anything, I am in danger of telling the truth about the secret. I was terrified of my gifts; they led me to reveal that I was intelligent, and that was dangerous. I had learned very early in my family of origin that my intelligence had to be hidden. I dared not reveal that I had a different internal purpose or identity than others in my family did. I had to have been gifted as a child, but one of my dearest sisters, when I began to reveal my gifts publicly, said in bewilderment: "Where is all this coming from? How are you doing this?" She had no prior knowledge of my potential.

It was also in 1975 that I began to be consumed by thoughts of putting my face in feces, eating feces, smearing feces on my arms, especially when I sang at the Lutheran church I was then attending. This filled me with shame. How could I share this with anyone? I thought it was just one more thing that demonstrated how unworthy I was. People in the congregation would tell me how they had been moved to tears by the power of my singing, yet I could not enjoy it myself because of my distorted thoughts. In 1994 I shared this with my therapist. He told me that it sometimes happens to those who think they are unworthy of success. There is a part of myself that wants to hurt my efforts toward success by flooding my mind with these scatological, or obscene, thoughts. I now know this was merely another symptom of the abuse I had suffered, but until I learned this, I hid these secret thoughts from everyone. (I was to experience these scatological thoughts while singing in the magnificent chorus at the Bahá'í World Congress in 1992 also. Here I felt moved to the height of spirituality, with tears running down my face, but the beauty was marred, probably by the internal eunuch who judges all desire to sing as sinful.)

I started dating the man who was to become my second husband in 1977. I had been aware of John as a member of my church for a long time, but had always thought he was married. On going to a church retreat in a nearby city, I saw that he was placed in the singles group. After I found out that he was single, I asked him to my home for Sunday dinner. He refused. I invited him to dinner or a movie every couple of weeks for about six months, and he continued to refuse. I prayed to God and decided that I was going to ask John one more time, and if he said no, I was going to become a member of another church, because there was no one else at the church I was interested in dating. I called him up and he said no. I hung up the phone and said, "That's that!" He surprised me by calling back in twenty minutes and inviting me to a play. We dated for two years and married in 1979.

A Married Woman with a Dilemma

Now that I had spoken the vows of fidelity, I had a dilemma. I was still the same unhealed person who was acting out a pattern of seduction, easy familiarity, and availability. There was still one man in my life with whom I was acting very provocatively and others I was trying to attract. My anxiety kept increasing. I could not have it both ways. But I still resisted engaging in ongoing therapy. I did not see a connection yet between my behavior and the sexual abuse.

Six months after our wedding, I received a wonderful lesson in the form of a marriage encounter weekend, during which my spouse, John, and I shared intense feelings for three days. This was when I finally began to trust my spouse enough to tell him about the sexual abuse I had experienced as a child. I had not told him before because I thought he would reject me for being depraved and evil. I fantasized that he would either leave me or have me locked up for being crazy. "Now I understand why you wrote your Skylark story. I couldn't figure it out before; but now it fits," he responded. And at that point he began to offer even more support than he had before. My faith increased dramatically! I had the acceptance of my husband, the person most dear to me. My desire to change deepened from that moment on.

The marriage encounter helped me to internalize the concepts about feelings that I had been learning. It was the first time that I had shared feelings openly and verbally with another human being, the first time I had felt truly heard by another human being, the first time I had truly listened to the feelings of another human being. It was an awakening!

However, something strange happened after the weekend of sharing feelings. I felt something wrong under the surface of my consciousness. I had no words for it. I ran into the bedroom. I tried to move my mouth, but it felt paralyzed. The closest I can come to describing the "something wrong" is that I thought my whole mind and body were going to explode. I opened my mouth, but nothing would come out. My throat constricted. I opened my mouth again, and an indescribable wounded sound was released. My husband came into the room and held me. I couldn't tell him what I was experiencing, but for the first time in my life, I didn't feel alone. This was a monumental turning point for me. Someone was there to hold me, to mark this moment in time as different for me; it was a necessary step on my path toward wholeness. Being held there, then, was a moment of trust. I began to cry. I said, "John, I'm so afraid."

I thought, "What kind of fear is this?" I had felt fear before. I had experienced an adrenalin rush before. But this terror was something different. I came to believe that this was the terror of the sexualized child that she couldn't express verbally. I was now conscious of her fear, her muteness and powerlessness. I began to reassure her when I sensed her terror.

I went to another retreat at Augsburg College in Iowa. During communion at the altar of the chapel a man from my church propositioned me! At the very altar of God! I was no longer safe at church! I was ricocheting off the walls emotionally now! I know I had done nothing to encourage this man. I was bewildered.

I began to be consumed with what I call an awareness of blind fear. I would awaken at 1, 2, or 3 A.M. with anxiety attacks, not knowing why. Then I would just get back to sleep only to reawaken at 4:30 for the day, getting only four hours of sleep or less per night—a symptom of severe depression. I prayed non-stop when I awoke. I prayed at work. I prayed on the way home from work.

I began feeling rage against the man who was encouraging inappropriate behavior in me. I began to fantasize that I would ram into his car with my car whenever I saw it. Where was this coming from? I began feeling rage because I was responding seductively. I would say "no" to him mentally twenty or more times a day, telling myself I would not engage in the "turn-on/come on" behavior, then participate in the behavior whenever I visited his city. This caused my conflict of values to kick in even more strongly. I lived in a state of intense anxiety over trying to identify what was "right" or "wrong" behavior. There were so many worldly standards to choose from, yet none of them seemed capable of resolving my conflict once and for all. An excerpt from my journal at the time expresses the conflict and confusion I was experiencing:

Fidelity and righteousness—why can't I make up my mind? Is this behavior wrong or isn't it? Is it this hard for everyone to be "good"? What is my standard? What is God's standard? What is so difficult about this decision? Why do I have to make it daily and even more often? Why do my sisters know right from wrong and I don't? Why does certainty always seem to elude me on this question?

I began to pray for fidelity and righteousness. Then, one day while I was riding my bicycle, my thoughts turned to this other man again in a powerful fantasy. Only this time the thoughts were interrupted by a powerful thought that literally blasted through my mind. "Be righteous for the sake of God!" I interpreted the thought in this way: I was to set right my behavior. I was to pursue rectitude of conduct. Out of consideration and regard for God I was to be righteous; meaning without guilt, fault, or blame. Not for myself, nor for my husband; but for God! The concept of obedience to authority crystallized in my mind. It was a powerful revelation. Righteousness; just the word was healing. I grabbed it like a raft in a whirlpool, not knowing whether there was any way out of the whirlpool.

For six months I was in agonizing conflict while I clung in prayer to the concept of righteousness. I was consumed by the need to find an answer to my conflict. I wanted to have no doubt about what behavior was correct. I didn't want to even think inappropriately. (I would later discover that this was impossible.) And at the end of six months, something happened that made me wonder if God had answered my prayers; a Bahá'í reentered my life.

Because of the ongoing relationship with my new Bahá'í friend, I was encouraged to reconnect with Bahá'u'lláh and searched a copy of Gleanings from the Writings of Bahá'u'lláh for the one verse that had for some reason remained in my memory for 10 years. I opened the book at the beginning and went page by page, scanning hopefully. I found the verse I was looking for: "Say: set ye aside My love, and commit what grieveth Mine Heart?"[10] I began to cry. I was grieving Him by my behavior? It was such a compelling reproach.

The whole passage was exactly what I so desperately needed to read. It not only convinced me that my inclinations were corrupt and that I needed to make the right choices, trusting that things would turn out right, but it also convinced me that this compelling, powerful Voice was the direction to which I should ever turn. The following extract captures the essence of the passage that spoke so directly to me:

> . . . Say: set ye aside My love, and commit what grieveth Mine heart? What is it that hindereth you from comprehending what hath been revealed unto you by Him Who is the All-Knowing, the All-Wise? We verily behold your actions. If We perceive from them the sweet smelling savor of purity and holiness, We will most certainly bless you. Then will the tongues of the inmates of Paradise utter your praise and magnify your names amidst them who have drawn nigh unto God.
>
> Cling thou to the hem of the Robe of God, and take thou firm hold on His Cord, a Cord which none can sever. Beware that the clamor of them that have repudiated this Most Great Announcement shall not deter thee from achieving thy purpose. Proclaim what hath been prescribed unto thee in this Tablet, though all the peoples arise and oppose thee. Thy Lord is, verily, the All-Compelling, the Unfailing Protector.[11]

The astounding revelation I had at this time was that I had permission to tell this man "no." I had Bahá'u'lláh's permission. I remembered also that I was to seek "righteousness for the sake of God." I became a Bahá'í in 1983, knowing in my soul that the power to heal lay in His Revelation. Just declaring my belief was frightening to me; I would have to face my husband. He was and still is a deeply spiritual Christian. Out of fear for my separating from Christ, he wept uncontrollably, and I started to waver, but I held firm because I knew of the nourishment I had found for my particular illness in Bahá'u'lláh's writings. I must add that the declaration did not bring immediate resolution to my dilemma.

I began to understand that my anxiety attacks were connected to disobedience to God. "And if he feareth not God, God will make him to fear all things; whereas all things fear him who feareth God."[12] I had been telling the man "no" mentally but not verbally. The hardest word for me to say out loud was "no." My weakest power for setting firm boundaries with others was the power of speech. Bahá'u'lláh was waiting not only for me to turn to a healing professional, but also for me to learn obedience to the law of chastity. I was to discover that the "fear of God" was a bounty and a power.

I had learned an outward, perfunctory "survival obedience" to avoid harsh punishment in my family of origin, but I had rebelled inwardly against true obedience. For someone like me, who had been severely traumatized by abuse, obedience to the truth of Bahá'u'lláh's Revelation would come in stages. The stages of obedience can be likened to stages of perfection. First came the lessons; then came expanded consciousness, new perceptions, and a period of putting what I had learned into practice; then came obedience in response to the new perceptions, with further lessons and tests to follow.

I knew that acting out sexually was immoral, but my entire consciousness needed to be retrained. The major focus of my life had been sex. My first memories were of sex. During my developmental years I had been robbed of my chastity, of which Bahá'u'lláh says:

> Purity and chastity . . . have been, and still are, the most great ornaments for the handmaidens of God. God is My Witness! The brightness of the light of chastity sheddeth its illumination upon the worlds of the spirit, and its fragrance is wafted even unto the Most Exalted Paradise.[13]

These words of Bahá'u'lláh would become my standard, my anchor, my guide when doubts assailed me and temptations threatened my stability. But the change that was needed—the retraining of my consciousness—did not happen overnight, and temptation still threatened my stability daily for quite some time.

Faith and Therapy Open the Doors

I have a physical problem that forced me to have a series of tests done at the Mayo Clinic in Minnesota. I was born with two extra bones in my neck. They are called cervical ribs. A doctor in Rockford thought that if they were removed, I would be relieved of the physical stress they caused. The doctors at the Mayo Clinic decided that surgery would leave me with too much scar tissue, which could cause even greater pain. During the process of examination, however, the doctors asked me if I had been sexually abused. I said no; I was still keeping the secret, still trying to get on with my life, still trying to be loyal to my family, still trying to protect my father. They ordered psychological tests, which indicated that I had been sexually abused and needed treatment. I had been found out. I could no longer deny that I had a problem. Yes, I needed to explore with a therapist the burdensome secret that I had been carrying for almost forty-five years. I came back home to Rockford and sought psychological treatment.

In 1985, after reading Claudia Black's *Adult Children of Alcoholics,* I became aware that I was an adult child of an alcoholic, and I began studying codependency issues. My father, three of his brothers, my grandfather on my father's side, and other family members had suffered from alcoholism. I began attending Alanon meetings to see how this fit into my illness. It was extremely helpful to know that the first step of the twelve-step program was to admit your powerlessness. I certainly felt powerless about my sexual behavior. It was in 1986 that I heard of a twelve-step program for survivors of incest and sexual abuse. Here is where I found the blessed release of speaking the forbidden secret out loud hundreds of times over a period of four years.

With one year in the support group for survivors of incest, I was feeling very brave. I was telling the secret! However, I had deluded myself that the secret was really "out," because I had never discussed it with any of the principle characters of this drama: my mother or my sisters. Sounds very strange doesn't it? That's the power of the secret. You know without being told that it is forbidden to talk about it.

It is important to note that every aspect of keeping the secret has to be consciously united with the tools of human intelligence and personality so that the person can achieve his or her true identity. Yet the ability to do this is discounted by a perpetrator of abuse and by a society that for centuries has protected the perpetrator, because our culture and others are based on the doctrine of original sin.[14]

I did not feel that I had permission to use these tools. The survivor uses every bit of being to keep the secret; so the focus of personality is skewed. We were created with many gifts within us. All of our abilities were meant to help us mine for those gifts. If our focus is to keep the secret, then we cannot develop our true identity, which connects us with our internal intention, our true purpose. If keeping the secret has become our singular obsession, then the goal of therapy has to be the freeing of the mind to achieve our true purpose, enabling the identity, the seat of our gifts, to develop. For the woman or man who has been taught to blindly obey authority, he or she must first feel that permission to use all human abilities and tools of intellect has been granted. I was to find that permission in Bahá'u'lláh's Revelation.

I had been taught to blindly obey an unwritten law that says talking about the subject within the family is forever forbidden. Mine was a whispered rebellion fomented behind the door of my support group where I was taking no risk to upset my mother, my sisters, and my aunts and uncles on both sides of the family. The thing about an obsessive secret once you start telling it in secret is that you feel as though you will explode if you keep it inside. Now you have another secret: you're telling the secret. And when you start telling it, even in a whisper, you begin to want to tell everyone you meet. The pendulum swings from absolute silence to the desire to shout it from the rooftop. You feel out of control. And the more you tell it, the greater your anxiety; because you could tell the wrong person, the forbidden person. The survivor would equate that with the realization of his or her deepest fear—ostracism from the family or the destruction of the family—and the horrible nightmare of the child could come true. It never occurred to me that telling the secret to the forbidden person was one of the keys to healing.

One day I was talking to my younger sister, and I accidentally said something about "what Dad did to me." I didn't intend to do it. It just slipped out. A rush of adrenalin hit me as she grasped the content of my words and almost violently grabbed my shoulders and asked, "*What* did Dad do to you?" I was rendered speechless for a moment by the swiftness of her reaction. Then began the outpouring of two hearts and memories as we compared notes. Now I had another secret. I had broken the unwritten rules. And when you break the unwritten family rules, you lose control of the secret. I found that I could not control my sister (thank God!). My anxiety heightened. This was in September of 1987.

Then in October, when I returned home from a vacation to Door County, Wisconsin, I found in my mail a copy of a letter written by my sister to our mother: a letter in which she poured out all the anger and animosity about the sexual abuse our father had perpetrated on us, naming me and disclosing what I had told her privately.

The secret was out, totally, forever. It was the beginning of hope for me. Because my sister had taken that step of bravery, I was able for the first time in my life, at 46 years of age, to tell my mother what had happened. I was terrified. For the first time in my life I felt I had permission to use my power of speech to speak the truth about the sexual abuse. I used the language of a child as I stumbled over words and grasped for ways to express myself. My mother listened quietly, reflectively, as she took it all in. She was full of questions, too. Another sister called, and another. My aunt in California called; she had known but remained silent at the time. We all began trading memories and sharing whatever facts we remembered. The secret was out in a big way. And my world had not fallen apart. I now felt I had permission to talk about the secret, and I couldn't stop talking. I began to write an account of my abuse, which became the foundation for this book.

I could now examine the secret fully. Because my power of speech was no longer blocked, other memories were able to surface. Thoughts that were forbidden were now unhindered because of my mother's encouragement. My ability to discriminate between right and wrong behavior increased because family members validated my father's behavior as terribly wrong. My sense of boundaries grew and with it my ability to protect myself.

My self-knowledge grew and expanded to include history that had been denied our family. We realized a greater unity than we had ever known. For the first time, we were pulling together as a family.

To understand the importance of this in the context of other survivors who shared their suffering with me in the support group, it must be known that some survivors do not have access to their memories for a long time. Their memory is using its power to keep the secret from them as well as from their family, everyone with whom they do not feel safe. Other survivors do not have access to their emotions. They fear that if they allowed themselves to feel the power of their emotions, they would lose control of them as well as the secret. And still others have been so abused that they express their speech, thoughts, and viewpoints in only indirect ways, especially when they are in great fear. No two survivors are going to experience the repression of their identity in the same way. I believe that is why there is no magical formula to heal the survivor. However, something "magical" happens when they do have freedom or permission to talk in safety about what actually happened to them.

Carrying the secret causes fragmentation and paralysis of personal power. My thoughts, feelings, perceptions, discernment, self-knowledge, reflections, identity, speech, sense of boundaries, imagination, questions, choices, memory, intuition, understanding, wisdom, and physical senses all had to be validated over and over as I revealed my secret.

The true purpose of therapy for me, and for so many others who have been similarly traumatized, is to develop, reassemble, and free one's personality and intellect. And the true task of one who wants to be obedient to God is to consciously develop control over one's will and abilities, thereby supporting one's quest for obedience. 'Abdu'l-Bahá, the eldest Son of Bahá'u'lláh and appointed interpreter of His teachings, states:

> It is certain that man's highest distinction is to be lowly before and obedient to his God; that his greatest glory, his most exalted rank and honor, depend on his close observance of the Divine commands and prohibitions. Religion is the light of the world, and the progress, achievement and

happiness of man result from obedience to the laws set down in the holy Books.[15]

In the process of getting therapy, keeping a journal, attending weekly support group meetings, and studying the Bahá'í writings, I told my secret hundreds of times. I uncovered unconscious, distorted beliefs about myself. I learned that, periodically, I would go into a trancelike state of dissociation. I became aware of so many things: a distorted thinking process that recurred from generation to generation in my family; decisions I had made as a child and continued to make as an adult that were no longer consistent with my changing belief system; my participation in and responsibility for others' seductive and inappropriate sexual behavior. I became aware that I was created noble, and I finally recognized God's law of chastity, which is a spiritual law that is designed to protect our psychological and spiritual well-being.

Another important part of my healing, learning to express my rage and anger in appropriate ways, prompted me to study anger and personal boundaries for seven years. Through this study I learned that I have spatial boundaries, as well as physical, sexual, property, intellectual, emotional, energy, monetary, and other boundaries, over which I had could exert authority. I began to specialize in writing and teaching about anger and boundaries in workshops, conferences, and at a community college. This did much for my self-esteem, as I began to realize that my gifts and experiences could be used to offer something valuable to others who were hurting. I invented the "Boundary Sculpting Game," which includes psychodrama techniques and role-playing. I created the video *Louis Timothy, The Giant, Invisible Turtle.* Louis Timothy had become a giant turtle because he was holding in his angry feelings, and he became invisible because he was afraid to tell others what he needed and who he was. The story won an award in London, England, and the video is now being used by Family Violence Shelters across the nation.

The more I reached out to help others with these tools, the more my ability to express myself developed, and the more I began to feel at ease as a performer. Today I can express my anger verbally, not two weeks or two hours after the fact, but at the moment that it comes up. I have also performed in two musical plays, singing and acting on stage. Performing felt wonderful, even though I had continuous anxiety attacks before, during, and for three months after the plays were presented.

With an expanded consciousness, new perceptions, new knowledge, conscious motives, and a strongly developed decision-making ability, I was finally able to say "no" to the man with whom I thought I was "in love," without changing my mind again and again. I ordered my thoughts and my behavior. I set boundaries. I knew what was expected of me; I had permission to use my own authority, and I chose to obey the commandments of God. I had tried positive thinking. I had tried exercise for the depression; I had tried medicine, yoga, progressive relaxation, vitamins, therapy, and finally obedience. Because my emotions were stabilized, I was able to work on other aspects of recovery that led to further growth and more complete obedience to the laws of God. I was also able to identify my distorted thought patterns, which helped immensely in reducing my depression. My obsession with the secret also subsided, and my mind was freed for the expression of my creative gifts. Door after door opened for me.

I had been the passive, compliant, blindly obedient woman but it did not work. God calls each of us to healing through obedience to His laws, which are there to set boundaries and limitations for our powers.

> O SON OF MAN!
> Wert thou to speed through the immensity of space and traverse the expanse of heaven, yet thou wouldst find no rest save in submission to Our command and humbleness before Our Face.[16]

I have learned as a result that acting in blind obedience does not release me from life's lessons and tests, but acting with personal power in submission and obedience to God's commandments does. There is a difference between a healthy, trusting obedience to God, which involves choice, and blindly abdicating the power of choice to a tyrannical authority. I have also learned that consistent obedience is the result of God's giving me several lessons that evoked a thousand new choices for which I am grateful and a thousand new perceptions that fill me with wonder. Suddenly, I experienced that "I get it!" feeling—that God was on my side and was helping me make new choices, not trying to punish me.

I have learned that there are stages of obedience that advance from imperfection towards perfection. Each stage must be judged according to its own merits, not as right or wrong, good or bad, but with three questions in mind: What has been learned up to that point? What has yet to be learned? And what is still blocking understanding?

How has my obedience benefited the sexualized child who still lives within me? For as long as I can remember, I have had a recurring nightmare. I would dream that someone was approaching my bed in the dark. Try as I might, I could not escape my bed. I was paralyzed, powerless. I tried to open my mouth to scream, but it, too, was paralyzed. A level of consciousness would penetrate my nightmare, and I could actually hear myself emitting nonverbal, guttural sounds even though my lips were sealed tightly. Yet I couldn't wake myself sufficiently during the dream to end this terror. I would awaken later, drenched with sweat, exhausted, and fearful of going back to sleep. I interpret this dream as an expression of the sexualized child's powerlessness.

In 1993, when I was 52 years of age, the dream recurred, I believe, for the last time. Once again the terror began to build as a figure approached my bed in my dream. Once again my mouth was sealed tightly as the desperate guttural sounds created a disturbing level of consciousness within my sleep. Then, incredibly, I sat bolt upright in my sleep and screamed a piercing "NOOOOOOOOOOOO!" It echoed through decades of silence, exploding through the lips of a child who had finally been empowered to put a word to her preverbal rage: "NO!"

My husband awoke and comforted me. The new ending to my dream changed me. In that moment I felt reborn. I had regained control over myself through obedience to the will of God. I realize now that my sexualized child could not have achieved stability until I had fully genuflected to God and chosen obedience to the law of chastity. That tiny, undeveloped entity has been empowered, through my obedience, to say "no!" Once I knew the laws, accepted them consciously, put them into practice, and finally stopped changing my mind, she learned to submit in trust to the internal boundaries I was setting for her because I became consistent mentally and behaviorally in all circumstances. Thus reparented, she was enabled to express her authority of self, and I was able to integrate all the component parts of my identity: what I think, feel, believe, imagine, say, am, desire, and do, with obedience to the Covenant of Bahá'u'lláh governing each component.

God has retrained His child. He took me from the developmental stage of a child to maturity, and taught me the morals that my own father was incapable of teaching, instructed me so that the abilities I was endowed with would emerge, then gave me permission to use my powers with authority. And in those acts He has proven to me that He was faithful to my wounded father, who was horribly abused by his father as well. God kept His Covenant with me as He keeps His Covenant with all.

> Among the safeguards of the Holy Faith is the training of children, and this is among the weightiest of principles in all the Divine Teachings. Thus from the very beginning mothers must rear their infants in the cradle of good morals—for it is the mothers who are the first educators—so that, when the child cometh to maturity, he will prove to be endowed with all the virtues and qualities that are worthy of praise.[17]

> Know that this matter of instruction, of character rectification and refinement, of heartening and encouraging the child, is of the utmost importance, for such are basic principles of God. . . . Thus will be kindled the sense of human dignity and pride, to burn away the reapings of lustful appetites. Then will each one of God's beloved shine out as a bright moon with qualities of the spirit, and the relationship of each to the Sacred Threshold of his Lord will not be illusory but sound and real, will be as the very foundation of the building, not some embellishment on its facade.[18]

I became responsible for retraining this sexualized child. I was supported unknowingly through this struggle by my mother, sisters, employer, husband, children, therapist, the Bahá'í community, and my own inner desire to strengthen my inherent nobility. To say that I am grateful sounds so inadequate. But I am grateful, and I praise God for His bounty and grace. I praise Him especially for the Revelation of Bahá'u'lláh, Whom I recognize as the Manifestation of God for the age in which we live. Without this Revelation, I would never have found my path to healing.

Chapter 2

What Is Trauma? Defining the Many Forms of Abuse

Introduction

It is significant that, "The Ancient Beauty consented to be bound with chains that mankind may be released from its bondage."[1] Its importance lies in the fact that upon this act of submission to the Will of God, a model for all, rests the character development of those who are straying from the straight path because of trauma in their early years. We have a responsibility to develop and refine our character, to educate ourselves, and to make conscious choices beyond our early training and conditioning, even though we were treated unjustly as children. Children have very little control over what is done to them; as adults, our opportunities are very different.

When I read about the abuses Bahá'u'lláh endured, I am heartened because I see that, while He experienced trauma, sorrow, abasement, and manifold afflictions, He assured us that it was to ensure the freedom, liberty, abiding joy, and prosperity of humanity. Those of us who have been traumatized need a visible metaphor for embracing liberty, joy, and prosperity. The image of Bahá'u'lláh in chains, valiantly and triumphantly rising above forty years of abasement to be the instrument of Revelation, provides that moving metaphor.

Very few of us have a life that resembles a flourishing rose garden; at most, our lives are bittersweet simply because we count among our family and friends those who suffer daily sorrow and upheaval, or we ourselves may be suffering in some way. Some of us may even have endured the kind of childhood trauma I describe in chapter 1. There are, however, many other kinds of trauma that plague us, such as the fearsome trauma that comes to war veterans who are victims of post-traumatic stress disorder; the inability to trust after having experienced rape; or adults and children who are terrorized by stray bullets in a violent neighborhood or war zone.

Although there is a tremendous variety of trauma and abuse that exists in our world, this chapter focuses on describing factually and objectively *childhood trauma*. I have no desire to discount the pain of those among us who suffer from other forms of tyranny. I honor their pain and I pray that they, too, will be released from it. What I focus on here is my own personal experience with trauma and abuse in the hope that this perspective will bring others closer to healing. Every story of trauma is different, every road to healing is different, just as Bahá'u'lláh's Revelation affects each person differently.

Recognizing Survivors of Abuse

Whether as a member of a Local Spiritual Assembly or an individual Bahá'í, we have all been acquainted with people from every strata of society and every culture who have been traumatized. Ongoing crisis that keeps them reeling from one disastrous situation to another makes them easy to recognize. The fact that some of the traumatized avoid entering community life should also be cause for concern.

Some survivors of abuse will manifest their trauma in obvious ways, such as self-mutilation or suicide attempts, and others in less obvious ways, such as "rebellion." For example, we may think it strange that an individual would want to be a Bahá'í while observing him or her forcibly resisting making a commitment to unity. Those Bahá'ís who have been raised in the embrace of love and bounty may not understand this type of behavior or even recognize it as being a result of trauma. For some of those who have experienced trauma, unity may represent the possibility of the overlapping of personal boundaries or the overpowering of their frightened, fragmented selves—a risk that will trigger great emotional upheaval within them, even in a loving community that we consider a "safe" place.

The kinds of behaviors we might witness in our communities range from violent relationships and battering, eating disorders such as anorexia, bulimia, or overeating, inappropriate sexual behavior and promiscuity, addictive behavior like alcoholism, drugs, gambling, and workaholism, as well as overt and covert depression, isolation, and estrangement. All of these behaviors offer clues that a person may have suffered physical, sexual, spiritual, mental, or emotional abuse.

Quite naturally, we want to assist them and their families. But a word of caution is necessary. Nobody else can tell someone that they have been abused and are in need of help for that abuse. It is the person who is manifesting the behavior who needs to come to that understanding. We should even be cautious about passing them a book that could "enlighten" them. Why? Because if memories are unearthed through reading about abuse without a support system in place, emotions long numb can suddenly emerge with no recognition of the cause. We can more safely and responsibly facilitate the process by perhaps saying, "Some people with these symptoms have been abused." We can look to the example of the Master for the keys to helpful attitudes and actions as we approach someone who appears to be acting out the pain of emotional wounds: be a willing listener, offer encouragement, and simple, undemanding kindnesses, ever careful not to hurt any heart.[2]

When Is Professional Intervention Needed?

How does one recognize when professional intervention is needed? Such help is indicated when symptoms interfere with the person's ability to live their life—for example, an ongoing crisis of flashbacks, anxiety attacks, and panic attacks related to the abuse, or an inability to function on the job because of a feeling of being "spacey" (going in and out of a trance). Other indicators that intervention is necessary are the revealing of relationship problems related to children or spouse, sexual problems, suicide attempts, or the abuse of children at home.

What is our role as Bahá'í friends who love and care for one another? If children are being abused in the home because a survivor of abuse cannot cope, then we need to seek justice for those children. We need to press compassionately for intervention. Justice will be served not by judging and condemning, but by seeking out a competent professional who knows how to work out abuse issues and work through traumatic memories.

Those who have been traumatized need to be empowered, and they need hope. The Revelation of Bahá'u'lláh can provide both. They need to grieve for what has been lost to them in order to resolve the trauma. Friends and trained professionals can take them through the natural sequence of grieving: denial, sadness, anger, and acceptance. Committed friends can let them know that someone is open to hearing about their anger and sadness. Individuals need to listen without judging, let them know there are places to get help, and act as their advocate if they suffer from a sense of helplessness that seems to debilitate them. Local Spiritual Assemblies need to listen as a merciful authority that will direct them toward professional help if it is needed and encourage responsible behavior that would help improve their self-esteem. They can offer to an individual authoritative consequences that will protect children or loved ones who may be suffering, because the behavior of the traumatized is self-destructive or harmful to those around them.

The Many Forms of Abuse

To understand such destructive behavior, we must first understand the nature of trauma. Generally, some type of physical, emotional, mental, sexual, or spiritual abuse causes trauma. Familiarity with the various categories can enable us to better determine how to serve the traumatized and act as an advocate for all who suffer abuse. Paying particular attention to abuses of children, they are summarized as follows:

> **Physical abuse** includes the striking, slapping, or hitting of a child on any part of the body, which results in bruises, welts, scratches, or broken bones. Sometimes the injuries are of such severity that there is internal hemorrhaging. The causes of physical abuse range from parental ignorance of healthy, nonviolent, ways of disciplining children, to batter-

ing the child while in a drunken rage or under the influence of drugs. **Physical neglect** includes deprivation of food, clothing, shelter, or medical treatment.

Emotional neglect and **mental abuse** occur when caregivers do not show an interest in the child, rejecting or verbally humiliating him or her. The child may be denied emotional responsiveness to its needs or denied the encouragement necessary for the development of his or her self. Leaving a child at home alone is a potentially dangerous form of neglect. Terrorizing or frightening a child into obedience is considered mental abuse, as is living with the possibility that a sibling or parent could be physically battered at any moment.

When children experience such emotional and mental abuse, it causes severe emotional and mental distress and disempowers them at a time when their self-esteem and identity are just forming. Furthermore, neglect and actual abandonment will traumatize a child.

Sexual abuse is the coercion of a person, a victim, into meeting the sexual demands of another person, the perpetrator. This kind of abuse can damage one's self-esteem, one's relationships with others, one's sexual development, one's trust in others, and one's ability to achieve success. Such abuse is often associated with disorders such as overeating, bulimia, anorexia, and chemical dependence. Sadly, it is not uncommon for children who are abused in other ways—and are thus starving for affection and attention—to be abused sexually, because they are easily coerced into meeting the demands of the perpetrator, who plays on their trust and vulnerability.

Incest is a form of sexual abuse inflicted upon a child by a parent, or other near relative, that can be broadly defined to include anything from sexual overtones, to forcing a child to look at pornography, to actual intercourse, sodomy, or other forms of sexual activity.

> **Emotional incest** is difficult to define because it can be far more subtle. For example, parents who openly talk about specific sexual acts in front of their children create an atmosphere of emotional incest. Chronic nudity or nudity at inappropriate times is also abusive. Children who are forced to listen to or watch caretakers or other adults having sex with each other are being abused. Hearing adults call each other sexual names is also traumatizing, as is living with the daily threat of personal sexual abuse when observing the sexual abuse of a sibling.

Whatever the circumstances of the abusive treatment, the abused child usually internalizes a distorted belief system that is based on the idea that he or she is worthless, guilty, and blameworthy. If victims of sexual abuse interpret their own participation in the abuse as having been willing, or even because they experienced pleasure, they may blame themselves instead of the perpetrator. "If only I hadn't seduced him." "If only I hadn't worn shorts to the picnic." "It was my fault, I got in bed with her." This type of thought process has to be revealed for what it is: absolution of the responsibility of the perpetrator of abuse.

The Result of Abuse: The Deprivation of Power

The end result of physical, sexual, spiritual, emotional, and mental abuse is that it disempowers the victim. Any kind of tyrannical or oppressive behavior disempowers. In society, tyranny can be defined as any arbitrary use of authority that is unchecked by legitimate laws or constitutional limits. In society, victims of tyranny, authoritarianism, or oppression are not allowed to receive their due rights within the social contract, and in the process of using their energy to develop mechanisms of defense to cope with this abuse, they lose the power to develop fully and exercise appropriately the capacities which would allow them to become mature, contributing members of society in the future.

Parents who think that their parenting methods are above the law, or who feel they are not accountable to a higher authority, may subject their children to authoritarian or oppressive abuse which robs the children of their right to seek truth, justice, safety, and other rights[3] that are clearly the birthright of every child. Healthy parents, like healthy governments, operate "authoritatively," or with a firm fairness on behalf of their children to insure that all members of the family are able to carry out their responsibilities and receive their rights.

As the most important authority figures in a child's life, parents may tyrannize their children without even being aware of it in the same ways that tyranny was perpetrated on them as children. Children, for example, are not born racist, but this form of behavior, which goes against all codes of human dignity, human rights, and laws, continues to be passed from parents to children when parents continually make negative remarks about another race to their young children, or when children of one race are segregated from others. Such taught behavior distorts a child's image of reality and suggests that one group is more important than another. Children, who are highly attuned to issues of fairness even in their early years, may raise curious objections to these practices and are often further tyrannized by the final and most subtle category of abuse, *the disempowerment of children through language*. Their questions, observations, or healthy exploration may be stopped cold with any of the following messages:

> Don't think. Don't talk. Don't make choices. Don't lead. Don't be different. Don't be aware. Don't be intelligent. Don't ask questions. Don't be close. Don't need. Don't be a child. Don't be weak. Don't change. Don't be happy. Don't see. Don't set boundaries. Don't trust. Don't be you. Don't try. Don't feel. Don't know yourself. Don't be. Don't take care of yourself. Don't like yourself. Don't disobey or challenge authority.

This type of language, a sample of "the age old patterns of subordination,"[4] is a verbal attack on the personal powers that are meant to help a child develop the gifts he or she has within, powers such as comprehension, reason, empathy, insight, and willpower among others. This is the means by which parents with tyrannical belief systems continue, overtly and covertly, to erode personal power in adulthood and to perpetuate racism and sexism. It is in examining the inherent implications of this language in the context of the powers and virtues that are latent in humankind that the negative beliefs and values current in society will be discovered and exposed.

An Abdication of Power

People who have internalized this language are open to all kinds of boundary enmeshment[5] and violation, can be made to do anything, will put up with all kinds of inappropriate behavior, and will allow others to hit, beat, verbally abuse, intimidate, manipulate, or criticize them. They do not know how to say "no," cannot control the amount of food they eat, the work they do, the amount of exercise they do, or how fast they walk or work.

They need permission from others to read "new and different" books, change their minds, change their style of clothing, stop working, get rest, stay home when they are too sick to work, even to eat or go to the bathroom.

They can become confused and anxious if someone frowns at them or at no one or nothing in particular. They will work until they drop, starve until they die, eat until they become obese. They will work at someone else's pace until they are in pain or until they destroy their health or their body. Everyone else determines their choices, their food, their religion, their schedule, their work, their attitude, their feelings, even their shoe size.

People who do not exercise their personal power in an authoritarian belief system may be thought of by those in power as loyal, dedicated, talented, patient, or flexible, and are highly praised when they don't take care of their own needs and interests.

What they find, however, when they abdicate power,[6] is that they lose their spiritual and psychological balance.

The Paradox of Power

Abuse at the hands of authority results in a mistrust of authority, a belief that all authority is tyrannous, and that power is to be grasped at all costs or abdicated. Some of the traumatized become very controlling and want more power; some revert to anarchy; some become victims (as described earlier), afraid of using their personal powers; and others become perpetrators using power as force. How are they to trust that God is a just Authority, as are His Institutions of authority on earth? How are they to learn to trust their own powers and to learn the appropriate use of power?

A basic premise we find in the writings of Bahá'u'lláh is that we are all servants of God, with powers that are our birthright. We can seek authority to use our powers as we will, but Bahá'u'lláh calls the authority of self a "fleeting sovereignty," a "mortal sovereignty," offering instead to us His "eternal, imperishable dominion":

O SON OF BEING!
If thine heart be set upon this eternal, imperishable dominion, and this ancient, everlasting life, forsake this mortal and fleeting sovereignty.[7]

O CHILDREN OF VAINGLORY!
For a fleeting sovereignty ye have abandoned My imperishable dominion.[8]

O CHILDREN OF NEGLIGENCE!
Set not your affections on mortal sovereignty and rejoice not therein. Ye are even as the unwary bird that with full confidence warbleth upon the bough; till of a sudden the fowler Death throws it upon the dust, and the melody, the form and the color are gone, leaving not a trace. Wherefore take heed, O bondslaves of desire![9]

Know, therefore, O questioning seeker, that earthly sovereignty is of no worth, nor will it ever be, in the eyes of God and His chosen Ones.[10]

While He cautions us about seeking a "mortal and fleeting sovereignty," Bahá'u'lláh offers riveting and copious examples throughout His Revelation of the powers of the servant, calling human beings "the supreme Talisman."[11] A talisman is an object that is believed to confer power and protection upon its bearer. In order for a person to mature spiritually, he or she must understand two things: one, that these powers must be developed for the purpose of service to humankind;[12] and two, that all power is subjected to the guidance of the God-ordained Institutions established by Bahá'u'lláh, their purpose being to protect the peoples of the world from tyranny and oppression and to guide them to unity and prosperity.[13]

The Bahá'í community, too, plays a large role in the healing of its members. In its truest character, it offers generous amounts of grace and compassion for the pain and ailments the traumatized suffer. For it is in the community where the cry of despair is first heard and the gates of reunion with God's people are first opened. And community is where we are led safely back to trust God's Authority.

Further Reading on the Subject of Abuse

For those who wish to delve a little deeper than this brief summary of abuse, I suggest reading *Outgrowing the Pain* by Eliana Gill; *Secret Survivors* by E. Sue Blume; *The Courage to Heal* by Ellen Bass and Laura Davis; and *Inside Scars* by Sheila Sisk and Charlotte Foster Hoffman. For an introduction to family dynamics, there is *The Family and Healing the Shame that Binds* by John Bradshaw. To understand the roots of violence, consider the following titles by Alice Miller, a Swiss psychoanalyst: *For Your Own Good* and *Thou Shalt Not Be Aware*.

Chapter 3

Tyranny, Power, and the Authority of Self

O OPPRESSORS ON EARTH!
Withdraw your hands from tyranny, for I have pledged
Myself not to forgive any man's injustice. This is My
Covenant which I have irrevocably decreed in the preserved
tablet and sealed with My seal.[1]

Tyranny

In a world that has become as desensitized to acts of tyranny as it
has to immorality, the dawning of justice in the face of such acts
comes as a brilliant contrast to the darkness that surrounds us. It
is difficult for many under the yoke of oppression to believe that
any authority could be compassionate or just. Some have even
developed a fatalistic response to their daily trauma, or a jaded,
cynical attitude toward God because they believe He permits
such violence. Others believe that the tendency to violence is an
inherent condition in humanity, causing a "paralysis of will."[2]

The masterful principles of justice and unity that Bahá'u'lláh
has brought—the equality of women and men, the elimination
of racism, the oneness of humankind, God, and religion, the
eradication of the inordinate disparity between the rich and
poor, the elimination of unbridled nationalism, the abolition of
war, and the cause of universal education—one and all speak to
the needs and desperation of those who have lost hope, and shed
light on the causes of oppression. With the principles in conjunc-

tion with the problems, the Universal House of Justice says we can find the solutions: "There are spiritual principles, or what some call human values, by which solutions can be found for every social problem."[3] They also encourage leaders of governments and all in authority that they: ". . . would be well served in their efforts to solve problems if they would first seek to identify the principles involved and then be guided by them."[4]

The problems of violence, oppression, and injustice affect all of us. When the minds and hearts of those in positions of power and authority, whether they are parents, teachers, employers, priests, or rulers, are laden with distorted beliefs of racism, sexism, prejudice, and selfishness, their rules and styles of governing will result in tyranny and oppression. For these reasons it is understandable that the world has become distrustful of power yet is lamentably in need of responsible individual power, as well as the power of a just and compassionate authority. Bahá'u'lláh writes:

> Justice is, in this day, bewailing its plight, and Equity groaneth beneath the yoke of oppression. The thick clouds of tyranny have darkened the face of the earth, and enveloped its peoples.[5]

Further He writes,

> They that perpetrate tyranny in the world have usurped the rights of the peoples and kindreds of the earth and are sedulously pursuing their selfish inclinations.[6]

As Bahá'ís we seem to separate ourselves from this description of tyranny. After all, this has to do with oppressive kings, dictators, and the ravages of war, doesn't it? Not entirely. There is a much broader application of the concept of tyranny than those of which we are consciously aware. As we reduce this large-scale concept of tyranny and bring it home to our families, neighborhoods, and cities, we then see that tyranny is reflected in the beating and sexual abuse of children, the battering of men and women, and in the withholding of good jobs and housing because of prejudice.

The dictionary defines "tyranny" as absolute power exercised unjustly or cruelly. It is the use of power to take power away from others. It is denying the worth of women, men, and children and thereby silencing their voices. It is denying education to anyone because of racism, classism, greed, or substance abuse.

Tyranny may be seen as depriving a child of the opportunity for righteousness and chastity, because it is difficult to substantiate perpetration of sexual abuse. It is also saying that a woman "asked for it" when she was raped because of the way she was dressed, and excusing the man's behavior completely. It may be seen as the absolute enforcement of rules, without taking human need into consideration. It is forcing a "role" upon a human being and not allowing him or her to develop a true identity. Tyranny is preventing the development of the self, thus turning a potential leader into a follower.

Bahá'u'lláh cherishes "the hope that the light of justice may shine upon the world and sanctify it from tyranny."[7] He further states, "There can be no doubt whatever that if the day star of justice, which the clouds of tyranny have obscured, were to shed its light upon men, the face of the earth would be completely transformed."[8]

The Local Spiritual Assembly has been invested with the authority to bring the light of justice to those who have been traumatized and oppressed by tyranny. The individual Bahá'í has also been empowered to share with the traumatized individual the regenerating message of Bahá'u'lláh.

This chapter seeks to create an understanding of how the component powers of the self can be arrested by oppression, tyranny, and trauma; and illustrates how Bahá'u'lláh's Revelation regenerates our powers so that we can attain spiritual maturity.

Because there are varying kinds of autocratic, authoritarian, and totalitarian systems pervading all societies today, humankind has not yet fully developed the powers necessary for supporting and enhancing spiritual maturity and authority of self. It follows that we cannot attain spiritual maturity if we are not conscious of our powers. We need to know what they are, how to develop them, and understand our participation in the process of others usurping our power; and we also need to recognize that a human being's station, requires that his or her powers— authority of self—be subjected to the laws of God and His Institutions of authority on earth.

'Abdu'l-Bahá teaches us that,

> Humanity has emerged from its former degrees of limitation and preliminary training. Man must now become imbued with new virtues and powers, new moralities, new capacities.[9]

For example, because of the principle of the equality of women and men, women are emerging from this former degree of limitation and are called to "enter the important arenas of decision-making" as "full participants in all domains of life."[10] It is further stated that women's power of decision-making is necessary to the next stage of our collective development. Therefore, the development of the power of volition must be defined for women and encouraged. Personal power must be placed in the hands of women, including the power of speech and the power to seek the truth, not just intuition and service for which she is traditionally known.

What Is Power?

In a world that is slowly emerging from the belief in male superiority and the subjugation of women, power is seen as forcefulness—the ability or official capacity to exercise control. The new world order as brought by Bahá'u'lláh, which has as one the goals of which is to break down the barriers that prevent women's ascent to equal status with men, calls for a new definition of power—one that takes into account the weak and the strong, the privileged and the deprived, and one that has special application for the traumatized from whom power has been withheld by tyrannical authority.

Josefowitz describes power as "effectiveness: the ability or capacity to act or perform effectively. This broader concept of power includes the capacity (the role) and the ability (the competence) to get things done by either influencing others or having access to resources. It also includes the idea of granting more autonomy to those with less power."[11]

Those who have been traumatized from childhood have suffered from powerlessness. Women and children especially have suffered the humiliation of being treated as property. An absolute controlling power has been used wrongfully over their minds, bodies, and spirits. Not understanding their powers, they have not known how to take them back without resorting to irrational behavior, forcefulness, or control.

We need to know the many faces of tyrannical authority and how it strips us of our powers. We also need to know with firm conviction that Bahá'u'lláh's Revelation restores the powers that tyranny has sought through the ages to keep from us. For every aspect of tyrannical authority there is a Bahá'í principle or teaching that nullifies its abusive power.

Bahá'u'lláh has provided the means of healing and protection through the principles of gender equality and consultation. Add the power of utterance and woman has power to protest abuse and give voice to what she has suffered behind a closed door.

A letter written on behalf of the Universal House of Justice states,

> The use of force by the physically strong against the weak, as a means of imposing one's will and fulfilling one's desires, is a flagrant transgression of the Bahá'í Teachings. There can be no justification for anyone compelling another, through the use of force or the threat of violence, to do that to which the other person is not inclined.[12]

Thus the hand of the violator is stayed by the protecting, uncompromising, and vigilant influence of our institutions.

As knowledge of these principles and teachings becomes more widespread, a vital first step should be for educators, authors, and those in positions of authority to prepare for the development of programs that will transform the deeply ingrained mental attitudes regarding violence and tyranny that are embedded in our society through such things as our language, child-rearing habits, and treatment of women. The quest for these sweeping changes will be carried forward by a just authority who, guided by the Revelation of Bahá'u'lláh, seeks to bring equity to those who have been traumatized and oppressed.

Just Authority

It becomes necessary then to define *just authority*, so that the traumatized may recognize where to turn in trust and become confident that such trust is justified. A rational, nurturing, and just authority treats all as equal with the right to dignity even though they may not have the same power, intellectual capacity, experience, or material status. A just authority based upon the Revelation of God and submission to His Covenant helps those under its care discover who they are through steadfast love, tolerance, and noncontrolling encouragement.

Aside from teaching children about God, the goal of raising children must be to transfer the concept of one's authority of self in measured increments as they become responsible and capable—so that at the age of responsibility, the child will know what his or her birthright powers are, be able to negotiate his or her needs in the world, and take responsibility for his or her own life.

Ian Semple has explored this concept in the light of five processes. The first is to accept personal responsibility and accept one's self as the ultimate source of authority; the second is to recognize personal fallibility; the third is to recognize a source of authority outside oneself; the fourth is to understand the requirements of the authority thus recognized; and the fifth is the exercise of judgment in carrying out these requirements.[13]

> The first is to accept oneself as the ultimate source of authority. The foundation for all development is to know oneself and to accept one's own responsibility for one's own life.
>
> In . . . a multitude of . . . passages, Bahá'u'lláh's first call to us is not to obey, but to use our minds, to judge fairly, to recognize, and then to believe and then to obey. He assures us that we have the capacity to recognize the truth and to follow it. That ultimate authority resides in ourselves is true for any human being, whether he understands it or not.

The second process is to recognize one's own insufficiency, learning that for a person to follow his own inclinations in everything leads to chaos in his own life and in society as a whole.

The third is to validate a source of authority outside oneself. This leads one to search for an external source of authority, for what is truth. When one thinks one has found such a source it is essential to validate it. To fail to do so is to sacrifice one of the most fundamental rights and duties of a human being.

The fourth is the process of understanding the requirements of that source of authority. Having decided that a source of authority is valid, and that one wishes to obey it, one can only put this into practice if one understands what that source of authority requires.

And the fifth is the role of judgment in carrying out these requirements. Unless one uses one's intelligence and good judgment in exercising obedience to authority, one may well end up doing the opposite of what it really intends.

All five of these processes require the exercise of one's reasoning powers. They are the negation of the concept of "blind obedience," and I believe that this concept of blind obedience is contrary to the spirit of the faith. Obedience for a Bahá'í, is the free exercise of one's will to follow what one believes to be right. Blind obedience is the abdication of one's free will.[14]

Blind obedience to authority is the abdication of one's authority of self, without choice, upon the explicit commands of an external source. This differs from divine acquiescence in which the authority of self and all of its accompanying powers are by choice willingly offered up out of love in obedience to the commandments of God. Many Bahá'ís who have been traumatized think divine acquiescence means blind obedience. It does not. Divine acquiescence "isn't reluctant obedience to a law that one disagrees with; it is full-hearted obedience to a law one cannot understand but knows must be right."[15]

With this foundation for understanding clearly what tyranny is, what constitutes just authority, what the limitations of the authority of self are, and the differences between obedience and blind obedience, the stage has been set for chapter 4, which defines and elaborates on the individual powers that have been bestowed on humanity by the Creator, so that every woman, man, youth, and child might serve the needs of self and humanity.

Chapter 4

The Powers of the Authority of Self

Noble have I created thee, yet thou hast abased thyself. Rise then unto that for which thou wast created.

—Bahá'u'lláh, *The Hidden Words*, Arabic, no. 22

Introduction

In earlier chapters, we have seen how devastating trauma and the negative use of power, or tyranny, can impact the individual and society. Among the many tools available to the traumatized in their healing process, one of the most important and comforting sources in this day is the Revelation of Bahá'u'lláh and the healing power latent within His writings. Within these voluminous writings are stored the tools for transformation, regeneration, growth, and healing. Within them lie the qualities and attributes of a healthy soul, as God has intended. As Bahá'u'lláh so eloquently pleads,

> The vitality of men's belief in God is dying out in every land; nothing short of His wholesome medicine can ever restore it. The corrosion of ungodliness is eating into the vitals of human society; what else but the Elixir of His potent Revelation can cleanse and revive it? . . . The Force capable of such a transformation transcendeth the potency

of the Elixir itself. The Word of God, alone, can claim the distinction of being endowed with the capacity for so great and far-reaching a change.[1]

Abuse, and its damaging effects, can hinder the progress of the soul. Bahá'u'lláh refers to the creation of humanity as "noble," and the debilitating impact of traumatic abuse hinders that God-intended nobility. In this chapter, we will delve into the Bahá'í writings to discover the tools we need to regain that nobility and sense of true self that God has intended for us. This chapter provides a look at the writings from the perspective of healing and self-empowerment. It discusses the powers God has granted to humanity to enable it to draw ever closer to Him.

The *authority of self* refers to our own ability to command the many powers, attributes, and faculties of which we are aware and the other virtues that empower us that are too numerous to mention. The words "power," "faculty," "capability," "gifts," and "virtue" are frequently used in the writings of the Bahá'í Faith to represent power. It is reasonable to assume that most of the oppressed peoples of the world have not yet developed the authority of self. They perhaps have not recognized or developed their own sense of control over these powers and gifts that have been granted to them as human beings. We can be sure that those of us who have been traumatized by physical, emotional, sexual, mental, and spiritual abuse have yet to develop many of its component powers as well.

Authority of self can be defined as the freedom and ability to use God-given mental powers to make rational and moral choices; self-regulation of the emotions; and the right or permission to act independently with the understanding that one has personal limitations. To develop a complete understanding of the extent of our powers, and our authority to use them, we must be fully cognizant of our limitations and conquer our own misbeliefs or vain thoughts about who we are, why we are here, and how we can best relate to our world.

The conquest of self (the image of self we developed within the limits of our guesses about life and its purpose as we grew through our childhood) enables authority of self, the capacity to identify and develop our full array of potentialities, to evolve to maturity. Each of us is born with God-given powers. But until we learn to use them as our Creator has intended, they will not attain their full and proper use. Our own authority and control over ourselves needs to be connected to the greater Power and purpose for which our lives were created. The key to obtaining the gift of the full use of the authority of self is understanding and obedience to the Word of God, subjecting all of our powers to the authority of God and His divinely ordained institutions on earth.

A person often holds the "libertarian" view that his or her own "authority" is all that is needed. But authority of self does not mean free will. Bahá'u'lláh, while granting that God-given position of humanity as the apex of creation, has pointed out that the journey for man is to cross from the material world into the realm of the spiritual, which cannot be accomplished unless we turn to an authority higher than our own, the Manifestation of God.[2]

As we use our powers during this lifetime and as we develop our understanding of how to rightly use these powers and our God-given personal authority, we must consider the balance between our independence from others and our connectedness to others. In numerous places, the Bahá'í writings encourage us to be self-sufficient or autonomous of others in our obedience to God's commandments. For those who have been conditioned to follow religion blindly, this concept can be difficult to understand. Yet, the Báb says:

> Vouchsafe unto me, through Thy grace, what will enable me to dispense with all except Thee, and destine for me that which will make me independent of everyone else besides Thee.[3]

He states further:

> O my God, my Lord and my Master! I have detached myself from my kindred and have sought through Thee to become independent of all that dwell on earth. . . .[4]

If we are to become independent of all else but God, we will have to use our authority of self to accomplish that goal. If we have been taught to fulfill the expectations of others only, or if we have been traumatized at moments when we tried to assert our independence, then it will be difficult for us to "become independent of all that dwell on earth." We may look to others for permission for something as inconsequential as choosing our dinner from a selection on a restaurant menu, or as monumental as leaving a relationship in which we are being violently battered daily. Knowing what authority of self is and understanding that it is a birthright from God is the first step in regaining the independence necessary to change our situation from one in which we are treated as an object to one in which we believe and assert to others that we are noble and will never allow others to tyrannize us again.

To balance this independence, it is also necessary to state that authority of self is a "connected state." 'Abdu'l-Bahá wrote that,

> The beings, whether great or small, are connected with one another by the perfect wisdom of God, and affect and influence one another. If it were not so, in the universal system and the general arrangement of existence, there would be disorder and imperfection. But as beings are connected with one another with the greatest strength, they are in order in their places and perfect.[5]

While the emphasis in this chapter is on our powers, we must remember that Bahá'u'lláh says, "Regard men as a flock of sheep that need a shepherd for their protection."[6] This reminds us that we must never use the *authority of self* independently of God.

The scope of this book will not allow me to provide quotations for each power in detail, but I will provide further references to that power in the Bahá'í writings, definitions for each power, as well as how using it promotes healing.

The Power of Recognizing God (Truth)
This is a faculty that dwells within each human being that enables him or her to recognize God and His Manifestations, or the Messengers of God. Bahá'u'lláh advises us:

The first duty prescribed by God for His servants is the recognition of Him Who is the Dayspring of His Revelation and the Fountain of His laws, Who representeth the Godhead in both the Kingdom of His Cause and the world of creation.[7]

It follows, therefore, that every man hath been, and will continue to be, able of himself to appreciate the Beauty of God, the Glorified. Had he not been endowed with such a capacity, how could he be called to account for his failure? If, in the Day when all the peoples of the earth will be gathered together, any man should, whilst standing in the presence of God, be asked: "Wherefore hast thou disbelieved in My Beauty and turned away from My Self," and if such a man should reply and say: "Inasmuch as all men have erred, and none hath been found willing to turn his face to the Truth, I, too, following their example, have grievously failed to recognize the Beauty of the Eternal," such a plea will, assuredly, be rejected. For the faith of no man can be conditioned by anyone except himself.[8]

The Power of Discernment

Discernment is the ability to see and distinguish the difference between good and evil, degrees of perfection and imperfection, light and darkness, and truth and falsehood. Empowered by discernment, one makes choices that reflect spiritual values. We not only have to discern right from wrong, we have to know *why* it's right or wrong. We can gain this understanding from the Bahá'í writings.

Discernment also gives one the ability to comprehend that which is shrouded or hidden in darkness. Bahá'u'lláh writes:

So great shall be the discernment of this seeker that he will discriminate between truth and falsehood, even as he doth distinguish the sun from shadow.[9]

Gaining the *power of discernment* means educating oneself about what constitutes abuse and chastity, and identifying the kinds of behavior, caused by trauma, that are inappropriate to spiritual and psychological health either for the individual or society. Discernment is supported by the power of inner vision, which leads us to "know the gem from the stone."[10] Discernment is strengthened with the power of will. Without the power of will, discernment cannot effect change. (See p. 77.)

The Power of Wisdom

The *power of wisdom* is the capacity to judge rightly in matters relating to life and conduct. It is soundness of judgment in the choice of means and ends and discerns inner qualities and relationships. Bahá'u'lláh elaborates on this:

> Above all else, the greatest gift and the most wondrous blessing hath ever been and will continue to be Wisdom. It is man's unfailing Protector. It aideth him and strengtheneth him. Wisdom is God's Emissary and the Revealer of His Name the Omniscient. Through it the loftiness of man's station is made manifest and evident. It is all-knowing and the foremost Teacher in the school of existence.[11]

For traumatized Bahá'ís, wisdom is the acknowledgment of "... whatsoever God hath clearly set forth."[12] This is the beginning of our healing. We measure our current state of abasement, whatever injustice caused it, against that which Bahá'u'lláh has set forth in the writings.[13]

Utilizing wisdom is often a difficult task, even for those who seem quite mature, but Bahá'u'lláh helps us recognize that true wisdom appears when consultation and compassion are present:

> The heaven of divine wisdom is illumined with the two luminaries, consultation and compassion . . .[14]

This shows us that we are able to openly discuss what is the wise course so that we might all benefit from the principles applied. Consultation and empathy help us look ahead for all who will be affected by any course of action that we think is wise to take.

The Power of Limitations

The *power of limitations* allows us to recognize that the self has limits, creating room within the limits to make some choices, knowing that self-regulation is ultimately an internalized process dependent upon our understanding of the Bahá'í writings. It is the ability to recognize and understand consequences for our behavior. "Every created thing will be enabled (so great is this reflecting power) to reveal the potentialities of its pre-ordained station, will recognize its capacity and limitations, and will testify to the truth that 'He, verily, is God; there is none other God besides Him.'"[15]

The faculty of shame, which guards us against that which is unworthy and unseemly,[16] and the fear of God are also a part of the power of limitations.[17]

The Power of Understanding

The *power of understanding* enables you to grasp the nature, significance, or explanation of something; to comprehend; and to make experience intelligible by applying concepts and categories, arriving at a result after being informed or educated, or through the process of consultation. To create greater understanding, the powers of utterance and intellectual investigation must be used (see pp. 70–71 and pp. 80–81).

> First and foremost among these favors, which the Almighty hath conferred upon man, is the gift of understanding. His purpose in conferring such a gift is none other except to enable His creatures to know and recognize the one true God—exalted be His glory. This gift giveth man the power to discern the truth in all things, leadeth him to that which is right, and helpeth him to discover the secrets of creation.[18]

Becoming free of the trauma is possible when each experience is understood as something that happened *to* us rather than something *we* caused. This is the value of therapy and consultation, which Bahá'u'lláh says increases the understanding.[19]

The Power of Perception

Perception is not only what we sense or perceive through our outer powers (the five physical senses), but also how we interpret what we see and experience. Perception is also understanding through the senses. Because perception can be clouded, and influenced by any number of factors, the *power of perception* must be teamed with the power of discernment. The danger is that our perception may be influenced by a multitude of negative emotions including resentment, hate, and irrational fear. On the other hand, positive perceptions can be made through emotions or virtues such as patience, courage, magnanimity, and compassion.

"The clarity of perception can" also be "clouded by self-interest and conceit."[20] Becoming aware of all these factors may be the process of purification 'Abdu'l-Bahá is referring to when He says, "Purify and sanctify the eyes that they may perceive Thy light. Purify and sanctify the ears in order that they may hear the call of Thy Kingdom."[21] At the very least, it is the "expansion of consciousness" that 'Abdu'l-Bahá says is so important. The Bahá'í writings help us fuse discernment with perception.[22]

The Power of Identity

Identity is being yourself and not someone else. It is the fact that you exist as a separate entity, expressing self-identity, and that you, as a single human being, are distinguished from others based upon your own attributes. It is acting according to your true self, without hypocrisy or constraint. The *power of identity* gives you the ability to firmly know who you are, what is important to you, what you think is right or wrong, and where you fit in this world. It shows you where your identity ends and the identities of your parents, spouse, children, friends, and others begins, so that you do not enmesh yourself in someone else's identity or allow others to enmesh themselves in yours. We have three basic needs as our power of identity develops: to learn that our identity (what we think, feel, desire, or choose) must be obedient to the Covenant of God, to be accepted by those who matter most to us, and to be ourselves.

Tyrannical authority says: "Mirror me. Give up your identity and absorb the role I prescribe for you." In contrast, Bahá'u'lláh writes,

O My servants! Could ye apprehend with what wonders of My munificence and bounty I have willed to entrust your souls, ye would, of a truth, rid yourselves of attachment to all created things, and would gain a true knowledge of your own selves—a knowledge which is the same as the comprehension of Mine own Being.[23]

When one's sense of identity is strong and clear, one is not afraid of losing approval, making it an excellent defense against peer pressure. Because the authority of self is an autonomous yet connected state, our identity is connected to all creation. Living in connectedness with others does not mean we give up our identity or individuality. We bring our gifts and attributes in cooperation and reciprocity to achieve that connectedness in an ever-advancing civilization. 'Abdu'l-Bahá has said: "Let all be set free from the multiple identities that were born of passion and desire, and in the oneness of their love for God find a new way of life."[24]

On the subject of self, the following was written on behalf of Shoghi Effendi:

Regarding the questions you asked: self has really two meanings, or is used in two senses, in the Bahá'í writings; one is self, the identity of the individual created by God. This is the self mentioned in such passages as "he hath known God who hath known himself", etc. The other self is the ego, the dark, animalistic heritage each one of us has, the lower nature that can develop into a monster of selfishness, brutality, lust and so on. It is this self we must struggle against, or this side of our natures, in order to strengthen and free the spirit within us and help it to attain perfection.

Self-sacrifice means to subordinate this lower nature and its desires to the more godly and noble side of our selves. Ultimately, in its highest sense, self-sacrifice means to give our will and our all to God to do with as He pleases. Then He purifies and glorifies our true self until it becomes a shining and wonderful reality.[25]

Harsh, judgmental attitudes toward a child's honest feelings, needs, and thoughts is criticism and censure of their power of identity. A healthy human being with a well-developed identity can deflect the criticism of others and take from it what has merit. But children haven't yet developed the inner strength to know that honest feelings of resentment or anger don't make them bad. Consequently, harsh criticism and judgmental attitudes can create a negative identity—one in which the child feels unworthy, unlovable, and unacceptable in the core of their identity when they express their honest feelings and thoughts. Self-esteem is defined as a favorable appreciation or opinion of oneself (i.e., identity). Separating feelings from behavior is important in that it is behavior that can be judged as "good" or "bad," not feelings. When dealing with behavior, we must make sure the individual is still loved, even though his or her behavior may be inappropriate. This restores and supports the goodness of their true self or identity.

It is interesting to note that insanity is defined in the *Oxford English Dictionary* as "a defect or disorder of the process of adjustment of self (identity) to circumstances."

Since one of the definitions of the word integrity is firm adherence to a code of moral values, integrity has special application to the power of identity. Integrity, or unity of identity, is being able to integrate or form into a unified whole all the component parts of your identity. This is difficult for those who have been traumatized. The "role" that was handed to them may be composed of what it is safe to think, i.e., those beliefs, values, and actions that are approved by tyrannical authority. They have never been allowed to choose their own moral values, so their identity is conflicted.

A conflict of values can be more correctly translated into conflict of identity. Our behavior conflicts with our beliefs; our beliefs conflict with our feelings; our desires conflict with our speech; and our fantasies conflict with the principles of the Bahá'í Faith. In other words, we can't be considered whole until all of the component parts of our identity are unified firmly into a code of moral values. Therein lies another meaning or layer to the principle of unity that runs through Bahá'u'lláh's Revelation. It is when we, individually, have unity of identity that we can achieve oneness or unity collectively. Unity of identity allows us to achieve singleness of aim, purpose, or action within ourselves and in the community. 'Abdu'l-Bahá confirmed this goal when He wrote:

> O God! Make our souls dependent upon the Verses of Thy Divine Unity, our hearts cheered with the outpourings of Thy Grace, that we may unite even as the waves of one sea and become merged together as the rays of Thine effulgent Light; that our thoughts, our views, our feelings may become as one reality, manifesting the spirit of union throughout the world.[26]

The more we seek unity of identity through a closer reliance on the Writings and bringing ourselves to account daily, the more our false self (in fact the only identity we have ever known, whether sexualized, dependent, materialistic, violent, victimized, or gender-confused) will be set aside and our true identity—remolded, reconstructed, and regenerated—will be empowered to step forth in unity with others. For the identity is actually an amalgamation, an integrity, of all the powers we are given by God, in their particular portions and limitations, and how we develop them and put them into service for the highest good.

We can achieve an identity as a servant of God. This is confirmed by 'Abdu'l-Bahá:

> My name is 'Abdu'l-Bahá. My identity is 'Abdu'l-Bahá. My qualification is 'Abdu'l-Bahá. My reality is 'Abdu'l-Bahá. My praise is 'Abdu'l-Bahá. Thralldom to the Blessed Perfection is my glorious and refulgent diadem and servitude to all the human race is my perpetual religion.[27]

Again He admonishes, "Follow the example of 'Abdu'l-Bahá in servitude to the Holy and exalted Threshold."[28] And who can ignore or forget the heartfelt command in the song we teach our children, "Look at me. Follow me. Be as I am," a phrase that likely came from pilgrim's notes.

A focused power of identity is essential to creating unity.

Unless one is sure of their identity as a servant of God, unity cannot be established in such places as the Nineteen Day Feast—the very purpose of which is unity. In a state of unity, true intimacy comes into being.

Intimacy is the ability to enter into connectedness with others without the fear of domination. It is the fusing of two or more identities into a whole through the process of self-awareness, self-disclosure, and trust. It is the moral integrity to commit to unity collectively without the fear of losing authority of self or its component power of identity.

Having self-awareness of the multiple identities that threaten to push aside the station of servitude, which is our true identity, is also necessary. And, finally, one has to be willing to commit to intimacy on a regular basis, since it has a nurturing quality and produces a calming of the soul. This is why we crave intimacy. Our soul craves to be calmed. Our soul hungers for unity.[29]

The Power of Utterance

The *power of utterance* can be defined as the exercise of the right and the opportunity to speak, describe, discuss, and explain one's truth, preferences, desires, opinions, and convictions. It includes the right and the opportunity to speak to the needs of self and others, to ask questions without fear, and the right to explore thoughts verbally with someone who listens without being defensive or distorting what is said. This power must be used conjointly with the powers of discernment and wisdom. Voice creates more knowing, and knowing, in turn, creates more voice. Verbal discussion helps to expand thinking and confirm the sense of identity. Silence represents an extreme in denial of self, and in dependence upon external authority for direction.[30] The critical and liberating power of speech in dialogue with others precedes the ability to act. "Man's treasure is his utterance."[31]

> O My Name! Utterance must needs possess penetrating power. For if bereft of this quality it would fail to exert influence. And this penetrating influence dependeth on the spirit being pure and the heart stainless. Likewise it needeth

moderation, without which the hearer would be unable to bear it, rather he would manifest opposition from the very outset. And moderation will be obtained by blending utterance with the tokens of divine wisdom which are recorded in the sacred Books and Tablets. Thus when the essence of one's utterance is endowed with these two requisites it will prove highly effective and will be the prime factor in transforming the souls of men. This is the station of supreme victory and celestial dominion. Whoso attaineth thereto is invested with the power to teach the Cause of God and to prevail over the hearts and minds of men.[32, 33]

The Power of Thought

The *power of thought* is the action or process of thinking and the formation and arrangement of ideas in the mind. It is an idea suggested or recalled, a reflection or consideration, an opinion or judgment, a belief or supposition with which to then reason, reflect upon, understand, act upon, or discard. Many of the traumatized, especially women, are afraid to reveal or speak their thoughts or opinions. This hinders the development of their identity and paralyzes their ability to act.

Thoughts can be spiritual or material. Many of the traumatized intellectualize as a way of avoiding strong feelings during therapy or intimacy. They "stay in their head," because to feel any emotion makes them feel as though they are losing their balance.

Sexualized thought—There are some theorists, both religious and psychological, who, based in "value-free" therapy, would lead you to believe that irrational and impulsive sexualized thoughts and fantasies are "friendly," neutral, or otherwise harmless. I strongly disagree. From the perspective of authority of self, those with weakened powers of cognition (self-awareness), utterance, hearing, discernment, volition, and limitations, are in grave danger of acting out their thoughts and fantasies. It is when these specific powers are developed that we can tell those whose thoughts are sexualized that they are harmless, because they would then have the power to refrain from acting on them.

'Abdu'l-Bahá stated that, "The reality of man is his thought, not his material body. The thought force and the animal force are partners. Although man is part of the animal creation, he possesses a power of thought superior to all other created beings."[34]

The Power of Reasoning

Reason involves evaluating experiences and drawing conclusions, which includes the right and the opportunity to discuss your own thoughts and point of view—including facts, interpretation of facts, and your values—in two-way dialogue or consultation, and in this way to inform, educate, empower, and discover reality. Only by reasoning aloud, without fear of punishment or threats, can the traumatized develop a strong sense of identity and benefit from guidance and support.

> Know ye that God has created in man the power of reason, whereby man is enabled to investigate reality. God has not intended man to imitate blindly his fathers and ancestors. He has endowed him with mind, or the faculty of reasoning, by the exercise of which he is to investigate and discover the truth, and that which he finds real and true he must accept. He must not be an imitator or blind follower of any soul. He must not rely implicitly upon the opinion of any man without investigation; nay, each soul must seek intelligently and independently, arriving at a real conclusion and bound only by that reality. The greatest cause of bereavement and disheartening in the world of humanity is ignorance based upon blind imitation. It is due to this that wars and battles prevail; from this cause hatred and animosity arise continually among mankind.[35]

Tyranny is perpetuated from generation to generation by blind imitation of traditional methods of child rearing that are in reality abusive. The freedom to investigate new methods of parenting creates new perceptions and new understanding, which lead to new choices as these new perceptions are explored through the reasoning process.[36]

The Power of Faith

This power is developed through consistent faith experiences derived from a nurturing family and social life which have taught us to trust in ourselves, others, and the unknown, or to trust in God. This is the "conscious knowledge" described by 'Abdu'l-Bahá.[37] It is useless to tell the traumatized that they must have faith or to tell them they would not have "these problems" if they only had faith. They must first and repeatedly be guided into personal and community experiences in which they begin to trust and believe that "things" will turn out all right. Then they will have the conscious knowledge that will support stepping out with courage. Intellect has to be conscious. Emotions have to be conscious. Physical pain has to be conscious, or they will doubt what their intuition is telling them.

If and when the traumatized can recognize these "internal alarms" and their power of limitations is developed, it will strengthen their *power of faith*. They will begin to have faith that they will not hurt themselves and that others cannot hurt them or infringe on their rights, because they have the power to set boundaries for themselves and others. Even more, they will be conscious at the moment others try to manipulate them, instead of two hours, two days, two months, or two years after the fact.

Be assured that Bahá'u'lláh's writings work towards helping the traumatized develop their power of faith through "confirmations." This is another form of faith experience provided for us if we did not learn to trust in childhood. Blind faith is not the answer, conscious knowledge is. Confirmation gives us conscious knowledge.

Bahá'u'lláh tells us in this quotation that the power of faith is necessary for creating unity:

> O contending peoples and kindreds of the earth! Set your faces towards unity, and let the radiance of its light shine upon you. Gather ye together and for the sake of God resolve to root out whatever is the source of contention amongst you.
>
> Arise and, armed with the power of faith, shatter to pieces the gods of your vain imaginings, the sowers of dissension amongst you.[38]

Cynicism and bitterness block the power of faith.

The Power of Imagination

The *power of imagination* is used to form a mental image or picture of something not present to the senses or never before wholly perceived in reality. Imagination is especially important to the development of our mental and spiritual gifts. We can imagine, as children, what we want to be when we grow up. Imagination can help us dream things into happening. Sometimes we will have to test imagination with other powers to see if it is helpful or harmful. If it is helpful, we can create something of value with it. If it is harmful, we will need to make responsible choices concerning imagination. If it is vain imagination, we can correct choices or redirect our thoughts and efforts.

Therapy can help the traumatized separate fact from imagination or fantasy. It often happens that reality is so terrible for an abused child that he or she creates a fantasy in which the parent is benevolent instead of tyrannical. The child uses the power of imagination as a defense to do this, which reveals that imagination has two aspects to it. It can lead us to truth or fantasy. Therefore, the power of imagination must be used with the powers of discernment, wisdom, reasoning, and intellectual investigation (see pp. 63–64, 72, and 80–81).

The power of imagination is discussed by 'Abdu'l-Bahá. He states, "As to the difference between inspiration and imagination, inspiration is in conformity with the Divine Texts, but imaginations do not conform therewith."[39] Idle and vain imaginations are mentioned quite frequently in the Bahá'í writings, but I will include only one reference to them here: "Protect us, we beseech Thee, O my Lord, from the hosts of idle fancies and vain imaginations."[40] The word "hosts" is very illuminating here. A host is an army, a great number; this illustrates how important it is to monitor our thoughts and to continue developing all the components of authority of self.

The Power of Inner Vision

This faculty allows us to attain direct knowledge or cognition without evident rational thought and inference. This includes quick and ready insight or intuition. The best way to handle intuition is not to assume you are right, but also not to assume you are wrong. Discuss what you intuit with others, search the writings for confirmation, or study the literature on the topic to determine the facts, to test your insight. Intuition can also be described as the inner voice, inner vision, and inner ear that helps us respond to that which is sacred:

> God . . . has created for us both material blessings and spiritual bestowals. He has given us material gifts and spiritual graces, outer sight to view the lights of the sun and inner vision by which we may perceive the glory of God. He has designed the outer ear to enjoy the melodies of sound and the inner hearing wherewith we may hear the voice of our Creator.[41]

The power of intellectual investigation of truth confirms and validates the *power of inner vision,* as does the power of understanding that comes from reading the Word of God. If verbally questioning authority is forbidden, we have no way to validate our inner vision and will doubt and discount it.[42]

The Affective Power
The *affective power* allows us to feel and be conscious of feeling, to manifest and be conscious of manifesting, to express and be conscious of expressing emotions, to be aware of the necessity to refrain from "emotional reasoning" (that is, selecting behavior solely on the basis of how one feels rather than utilizing all the components of the authority of self with which to make moral and behavioral choices).

A cautionary note about emotional reasoning: opinions, ideas, decisions, actions, and beliefs can arise out of pure emotion. A good example of the need to control and direct the affective power is the many fearful beliefs of those who are having anxiety attacks. For example, I was afraid to perform on stage. My recurring belief when I considered performing was that I would act out sexually, would be labeled promiscuous, and that someone would turn me into a prostitute. By challenging my fear and its accompanying emotional reasoning, I was able to test the veracity of my thinking and beliefs as well as my narrow opinion of other performers who were less inhibited than I was. Though I experienced severe anxiety attacks during the audition, throughout the rehearsals and the performances, as well as even two months after the show ended, I was able to perform satisfactorily. I made new friends and rid myself of a belief system that was self-limiting and unhealthy. This contributed to the development of my power of understanding. Because I had new perceptions with which to reason, I thereby came to new understanding of an art form that so many people enjoy and one that is important to my life work. Many traumatized persons need to form new understandings through the development of their emotional intelligence: gathering information about oneself in order to utilize all of one's powers to make choices.

If you have never read the Bahá'í writings with the purpose of discovering the emotions which Bahá'u'lláh expresses, there is no time like the present for this astounding discovery. His physical and emotional torment in prison, His deep sorrow because His own relatives turned against Him, yet His faithful submission to God for all that He was ordained to bear, and which He did bear without acting out with resentment—all are a lesson for us.[43]

The Cognitive Power

Cognition is the power of knowing. It is knowledge, consciousness, and acquaintance with a subject. The power of knowing taken in its widest sense includes sensation, perception, conception, as distinguished from feeling and volition. It is being able to know yourself (self-awareness); to use knowledge and awareness to form judgments; to make choices; and to know God. 'Abdu'l-Bahá writes:

> . . . that which is the cause of everlasting life, eternal honor, universal enlightenment, real salvation and prosperity is, first of all, the knowledge of God. It is known that the knowledge of God is beyond all knowledge, and it is the

greatest glory of the human world. For in the existing knowledge of the reality of things there is material advantage, and through it outward civilization progresses; but the knowledge of God is the cause of spiritual progress and attraction, and through it the perception of truth, the exaltation of humanity, divine civilization, rightness of morals and illumination are obtained.[44]

In order to begin the process of healing, the traumatized must gain the power of knowledge of the abuse; many of us have been forbidden to "know" we have been abused. Alice Miller, a Swiss psychoanalyst, has written an entire book on this entitled *Thou Shalt Not Be Aware*.[45] There are many who perpetrate tyranny by forbidding the development of the cognitive power. For example, the education of women has been opposed for centuries. 'Abdu'l-Bahá asks, "Why should a woman be left mentally undeveloped? Science is praiseworthy—whether investigated by the intellect of man or woman. So, little by little, woman advanced, giving increasing evidence of equal capabilities with man—whether in scientific research, political ability or any other sphere of human activity. The conclusion is evident that woman has been outdistanced through lack of education and intellectual facilities. If given the same educational opportunities or course of study, she would develop the same capacities and abilities."[46] The power of cognition, the power of identity, and the power of utterance are part of the strong foundation for unity and intimacy with God, self, and others.[47]

The Power of Will

The *power of will* is the exercise of authority or power, or the use of mental powers such as wishing, choosing, desiring, or intending. It is conscious choice. It includes control over one's own actions or emotions, and the highest form of will is aligning one's own will with the Will of God, as found in the Revelation of Bahá'u'lláh. Having eliminated all thoughts that are distorted and all passions and desires that are not based on moderation and discipline, the power of will affords the right and the opportunity to make moral and behavioral choices and to meet one's needs, based on one's understanding of the Bahá'í writings and submission to the Covenant.

> Some things are subject to the free will of man, such as justice, equity, tyranny and injustice, in other words, good and evil actions; it is evident and clear that these actions are for the most part, left to the will of man. But there are certain things to which man is forced and compelled, such as sleep, death, sickness, decline in power, injuries and misfortunes; these are not subject to the will of man, and he is not responsible for them, for he is compelled to endure them. But in the choice of good and bad actions he is free, and he commits them according to his will.[48]

Women especially, because of tradition, are expected to fulfill certain roles, such as chauffeur, cook, nursemaid, housekeeper, and so on, but the more she can utilize her power of will within the limitations of these roles, the more she can tailor her roles to her true identity. She will be much happier by doing so. One of the many causes of depression for traumatized men and women is the inability to control some measure of their life. By developing the power of will they can meet some of that need.[49] Alcohol and drugs can disable many of our powers, but especially the powers of will and discernment.

The Power of Memory
Memory is the store of things learned and retained from one's activity or experience. It is the faculty by which things are remembered, the capacity for retaining, perpetuating, or reviving the thought of things past. In many cases the effects of trauma can keep us from remembering vital information, skills, lessons, values, rules, plans, experiences, places, people, or events. Some adults have blank periods throughout the history of their childhood or adolescence, that are either temporary or permanent. Remembering unpleasant experiences or consequences can help us change behavior and the future. When the

powers of emotion, reflection, memory, imagination, and induction, among others, work together, they create an internal alarm that lets us know when we are in danger.[50]

The Power of Discovery

To discover is to obtain knowledge, to arrive through search or study at new knowledge, and to be the first to find, to learn, or to observe.

> Ponder and reflect: All sciences, arts, crafts, inventions and discoveries, have been once the secrets of nature and in conformity with the laws thereof must remain hidden; yet man through his discovering power interfereth with the laws of nature and transfereth these hidden secrets from the invisible to the visible plane.[51]

To experience the *power of discovery*, we have to assert our right to ask questions (the power of intellectual investigation of truth), and we have to develop the cognitive power, which may have been denied us. The root of the power of discovery is the power of understanding or the intellect, of which 'Abdu'l-Bahá has said:

> ... the intellect ... is supernatural. Through intellectual and intelligent inquiry science is the discoverer of all things. It unites present and past, reveals the history of bygone nations and events, and confers upon man today the essence of all human knowledge and attainment throughout the ages. By intellectual processes and logical deductions of reason this superpower in man can penetrate the mysteries of the future and anticipate its happenings.[52]

The Power of Reflection—The Meditative Faculty

The *power of reflection* is to think or consider seriously, usually in a meditative or pensive state. It is the concentration of the mind and the results of such consideration, communicated or not. Those of us who are hypervigilant are deprived of the power of reflection. If blind obedience has been exacted from us, we are afraid of developing the power of reflection. Some escape the meditative state and fall into a trance, which is called *dissociation*. The traumatized need to develop the ability to consciously stay in the meditative state. 'Abdu'l-Bahá says that "conscious reflection" is a power belonging to humanity.

> The source of crafts, sciences and arts is the power of reflection. Make ye every effort that out of this ideal mine there may gleam forth such pearls of wisdom and utterance as will promote the well-being and harmony of all the kindreds of the earth.[53]

The power of reflection helps strengthen our ability to recognize limits. True reflection ultimately leads to action, only after a reverent consideration of consequence, which is engendered by the power of wisdom. Galileo was said to have been "reflecting" day and night on the Old Testament Book of Daniel when he "discovered" the law of gravity, which is another indication of how many of these powers are interrelated.[54]

The Power of Intellectual Investigation
This faculty allows us to observe or inquire in detail, to examine systematically, and to search. It enables us to closely examine things in a quest for information or truth. Bahá'ís know this by a more common name—the independent investigation of truth. 'Abdu'l-Bahá writes:

> God has conferred upon and added to man a distinctive power, the faculty of intellectual investigation into the secrets of creation, the acquisition of higher knowledge, the greatest virtue of which is scientific enlightenment. This endowment is the most praiseworthy power of man, for through its employment and exercise, the betterment of the human race is accomplished, the development of the virtues of mankind is made possible and the spirit and mysteries of God become manifest.[55]

'Abdu'l-Bahá also affirmed that:

God has given man the eye of investigation by which he may see and recognize truth. He has endowed man with ears that he may hear the message of reality and conferred upon him the gift of reason by which he may discover things for himself. This is his endowment and equipment for the investigation of reality. Man is not intended to see through the eyes of another, hear through another's ears nor comprehend with another's brain. Each human creature has individual endowment, power and responsibility in the creative plan of God. Therefore, depend upon your own reason and judgment and adhere to the outcome of your own investigation; otherwise, you will be utterly submerged in the sea of ignorance and deprived of the bounties of God.[56]

This power is pivotal to the resolution of all kinds of tyranny, whether racism, sexism, or the variations of childhood abuse. When I chose to systematically investigate the truth of my childhood, and especially the years when I was a young mother, I found it not only helped my emotional and mental state—it would in fact become the means for each of my children to pursue their own mental health. The *power of intellectual investigation* confirms and validates the power of inner vision. Investigation of reality dispels darkness, curtails imitation, and helps to create unity.[57]

Knowledge emerges only through invention and reinvention, through the restless, impatient, continuing, hopeful inquiry human beings pursue in the world, with the world, and with each other.[58]

The Power of Induction
Induction is reasoning from the particular to the general: to infer by inductive reasoning. It is to draw a conclusion based on observation of particular instances and may also be based on emotions, memories, inner vision, intellectual investigaton of truth, and reasoning. One example is as follows: "Mom has been drinking alcohol. Mom is very angry right now. Based on

these observations, past experiences, and the feelings of dread and fear I am having right now, I had better stay out of her path. Better yet, I'll disappear."

The word "induce" means to lead a person by persuasion—or some influence or motive that acts upon the power of will—thereby facilitating change in behavior, attitude, condition, belief, or opinion. The "persuasion, influence, or motive" that acts on the will is a "power" called "principle," which defines truth and thus infers correct action for the individual and society. This is how all of the spiritual principles in Bahá'u'lláh's Revelation act upon the will of humankind to precipitate solutions to social problems.

The Universal House of Justice confirms this in *The Promise of World Peace,* where they explain that "The essential merit of spiritual principle is that it not only presents a perspective which harmonizes with that which is immanent in human nature, it also induces an attitude, a dynamic, a will, an aspiration, which facilities the discovery and implementation of practical measures."[59]

The Power of Deduction
Deduction is reasoning from the general to the particular. 'Abdu'l-Bahá wrote of deduction in regard to the power of discovery, "By intellectual processes and logical deductions of reason this superpower in man can penetrate the mysteries of the future and anticipate its happenings."[60] There are times when a person might be condemned for not being "logical," which could be a result of not being trained in inductive and deductive reasoning. These, of course, are powers the traumatized have been denied.

The Covenant of Bahá'u'lláh
Add to all of the above powers obedience to the Covenant of Bahá'u'lláh, and we have all the components of the "authority of self." Obedience to the Covenant of Bahá'u'lláh is acceptance, in essence, of God's power and authority, as well as the limitations and boundaries which God has set for us to preserve our

psychological and spiritual balance. The Universal House of Justice explains that:

> Covenant in the religious sense is a binding agreement between God and man, whereby God requires of man certain behavior in return for which He guarantees certain blessings, or whereby He gives man certain bounties in return for which He takes from those who accept them an undertaking to behave in a certain way.[61]

When these resources, the powers which are our birthright, are thwarted either by a tyrannical authority or as a result of living in an abusive situation, we do not have full access to reality. We are mentally, emotionally, and spiritually handicapped, because to use our resources or powers to the fullest would be to disobey authority. What we are left with are innumerable defense mechanisms that are ineffective and that thwart our ability to grow into the authority of self.

Conclusion: How Our Powers Are Interrelated

The analogy of the mind being like a computer also applies to how swiftly our powers move to support and interact with each other. We don't always recognize that it is happening. We just do it. By writing out a few examples, however, we can see how the process works.

For example, the power of recognizing God or His Manifestation is dependent upon the gift, or power, of understanding, conferred by God. God confers this gift through our creation, through which we measure the accuracy of our perceptions and the soundness of our values and beliefs. When our perceptions and beliefs are changed through reading the Word of God, we are said to have the gift of understanding spiritual truth to the extent that we change our behavior to conform to these teachings.

When the individual is denied the facts or given false information, or if others make choices for the individual, he or she is unable to develop the power of discernment. From this we understand that the power of discernment is dependent upon the power of intellectual investigation of truth. The power of discernment is also dependent upon the power of understanding and the cognitive power. We have to know and understand why something is right or wrong. I like to think of the Tablet of Aḥmad as a prayer for discernment, since Bahá'u'lláh wrote: "Verily this is that Most Great Beauty, foretold in the Books of the Messengers, through Whom truth shall be distinguished from error and the wisdom of every command shall be tested."[62]

The power of wisdom is developed by regulating or mastering the affective power. We develop those emotions, such as tolerance and compassion, that can assist the power of intellectual investigation. Emotional reasoning and selfish passions, however, prevent us from acting with wisdom. The power of discernment (knowing right from wrong) along with the power of imagination (being able to invent solutions to dilemmas) lead us to act with wisdom when we exercise our power of will. If the traumatized go into a trance, they are really immobilizing these powers that could help them escape from the abusive situation they are experiencing. Going into a trance indicates that the power of faith has not been developed. If the power of volition and other powers such as intellectual investigation and speech are withheld, then it makes sense that the traumatized person would escape by going into a dissociative state. This is helpful, comforting, and protective when we are extremely frightened and dependent children, but disastrous for an adult who has to drive a car, manage an education, a household, or a career.

If the power of faith is nurtured and modeled through faith experiences, it will enable the individual to work courageously on the development of their power of identity. Without the power of faith, the power of will cannot support the development of identity or life purpose. The individual would then be other-determined (determined by the will of others) rather than self-determined. Without the power of faith, discernment cannot evaluate perceptions. Perceptions would be discounted and feared. Without the power of faith and the power of volition, there would be fear and/or danger that one's identity would be usurped by others in the necessary process of unity. Entering into unity does not mean giving up the power of volition or identity. The power of faith is really a key power in trusting the development and use of many of the other powers.

The powers of utterance and reasoning are also vital to using our power of limitations. The traumatized may use their power of faith to set verbal limits and boundaries for self and others to clarify acceptable behavior. This is important because it is the means of stabilizing the affective power and the power of imagination.

The affective powers of hatred and rage can disable the power of imagination, which is a necessary foundation to problem-solving, discovering, and creating options for moral and behavioral choices. Also, combining emotional reasoning with untested imagination can create unbelievable and unnecessary anxiety.

The power of reflection is an important faculty for assisting the development of compassion as well as for regulating more negative emotions. To react without first reflecting would show the immaturity of our powers—even deprivation of powers.

And finally, when a person has a firmly developed power of discernment (understanding of right and wrong), the power of induction can work quickly with the power of reflection and the power of memory, which retains the knowledge of former inappropriate behavior on the part of self or others, to correctly imagine the consequences of choices he or she is considering acting upon.

> Man has also spiritual powers: imagination, which conceives things; thought, which reflects upon realities, comprehension, which comprehends realities, memory, which retains whatever man imagines, thinks and comprehends.[63]

These, then, are our God-given powers, for which 'Abdu'l-Bahá taught us to pray:

> O God! Refresh and gladden my spirit. Purify my heart. Illumine my powers.[64]

Those who are bereft of these powers and of the multitude of virtues through which we express them are truly powerless, above and beyond being consciously without power in the presence of God. Such powerlessness is the root of the anger the traumatized feel from being treated as an object. In chapter 5, anger will be examined in a new light—the light of Bahá'u'lláh's Revelation, to enable the traumatized to better express their frustration at the injustice they have received.

Chapter 5

Boundaries, Anger, and Cognitive Distortions: Stumbling Blocks for Those Recovering from Trauma

Introduction

Most of those who have been traumatized or oppressed are not only deprived of their powers, but are also developmentally delayed.[1] So it's not surprising that many do not know how to recognize boundary enmeshment (an unhealthy and uncomfortable infringement of one's person upon another) and how to express anger in appropriate ways. Further, because we are saddled with cognitive distortions (idle fancies and false imaginings)—some of them born of honestly trying to make sense of our world with limited powers, and others inherited from an uninformed family or society—we experience stumbling blocks to our recovery. Many undeveloped powers, however, are dormantly embedded in our cognitive distortions, and therein lies our hope.

How do our powers help us in observing and setting boundaries, as well as in the expression of anger? To answer that question, it is important to define boundary enmeshment, anger, and cognitive distortions. They are defined here, and following these definitions will be a more involved explanation of how they are linked together.

Boundary Enmeshment

is the uncomfortable and undesirable infringement and control of a person's identity, space, body, sexuality, time, energy, money, possessions, emotions, and thoughts, and their responsible freedom to express such. It is usually perpetrated by someone who does not recognize their own psychological, spiritual, and physical limits and does not know how to set limits for themselves or with others. The ultimate remedy for boundary enmeshment requires acknowledgment on the part of the violator along with the reestablishment of autonomy, privacy, safety, comfort, reciprocity, and unity.

Anger

is a natural feeling response, an internal alarm, that can assist you in making conscious moral and behavioral choices. Anger can exist under the following circumstances:

(1)   as a response to situations in which you perceive that you are being disempowered

(2)   as a realization that your value system is under attack (what you believe to be important, right, or sacred)

(3)   as a conscious or unconscious perception that your psychological, spiritual, and physical boundaries are being violated, which may result in a loss of self-worth if you have not learned that you were created noble.

Cognitive Distortions

are ten known and scientifically documented patterns of thinking that lead us into false imaginings and idle fancies because we do not use all of our powers. Bahá'u'lláh stresses the importance of being free from such distortions: "It behoveth every man to blot out the trace of every idle word from the tablet of his heart."[2] Cognitive distortions are significant irrational ways of thinking or errors of perception that prevent us from finding solutions when we experience boundary enmeshment or feel anger in relationship to others with whom we live and work. These distortions are identified by Dr. Aaron Beck as: all-or-nothing thinking, over-generalizations, the mental filter, disqualifying the positive, jumping to conclusions, magnification (catastrophizing) or minimization, emotional reasoning, "should" statements, labeling and mislabeling, and personalization.[3]

BOUNDARY ENMESHMENT AS A STUMBLING BLOCK TO RECOVERY

The traumatized have difficulty recognizing boundary enmeshment, not only because they are enmeshed in the boundaries of others, but because they allow their own boundaries to be infringed upon. Only when the authority of God is realized can the boundaries truly be defined. We discover through the Bahá'í writings that God, our Creator, has equipped us with certain powers of the soul and revealed spiritual laws and principles by which we can exercise authority of self to set boundaries with others.

When we understand that obeying the laws of God becomes our means of having protective boundaries, we eagerly receive them as a means of freedom from instability, depression, and shame. As Bahá'u'lláh states:

> Say: True liberty consisteth in man's submission unto My commandments, little as ye know it. Were men to observe that which We have sent down unto them from the Heaven of Revelation, they would, of a certainty, attain unto perfect liberty.[4]

> That which beseemeth man is submission unto such restraints as will protect him from his own ignorance, and guard him against the harm of the mischief-maker. Liberty causeth man to overstep the bounds of propriety, and to infringe on the dignity of his station. It debaseth him to the level of extreme depravity and wickedness.[5]

By connecting our instability, depression, and shame to boundary enmeshment, we become aware that our spiritual and psychological balance is dependent upon obedience to the laws of God. It is through setting boundaries with others, as well as respecting the boundaries of others, that we become aware that the laws of God and the limits He sets for us are a mercy to us.

> O ye peoples of the world! Know assuredly that My commandments are the lamps of My loving providence among My servants, and the Keys of My mercy for My creatures." "Say: From My laws the sweet smelling savor of My garment can be smelled, and by their aid the standards of Victory will be planted upon the highest peaks." "Think not that We have revealed unto you a mere code of laws. Nay, rather, We have unsealed the choice Wine with the fingers of might and power.[6]

> We, verily, have commanded you to refuse the dictates of your evil passions and corrupt desires, and not to transgress the bounds which the Pen of the Most High hath fixed, for these are the breath of life unto all created things.[7]

Once we transgress the "bounds which the Pen of the Most High hath fixed," we experience shame.

> Indeed, there existeth in man a faculty which deterreth him from, and guardeth him against, whatever is unworthy and unseemly, and which is known as his sense of shame. This, however, is confined to but a few; all have not possessed and do not possess it.[8]

Authentic shame is an internal alarm that is meant to restore the spiritual and psychological balance within us. John Bradshaw states that awareness of boundaries is necessary to our psychological balance.[9] Limits are like the roots of the tree. Its roots keep the tree in place. Without roots the tree will die. Just as without limits, we will die. Shame tells us we've exceeded those limits. And if we are of those who do not possess shame and do not experience it prior to or upon a transgression, we have the writings to alert us to the fact that we have exceeded our boundaries.

Roller coaster emotions and instability are indicative of our own heedlessness with regard to boundaries, as well as our unawareness that others have enmeshed themselves in our boundaries. It is the writings that bring us back to center when the pendulum has swung too far and we have gone beyond our limits (or rather, the limits which God has set for us).

It is the writings that define immorality and tyranny so that we can correct our course. And those of us who have been taught immorality through having experienced or witnessed force and/or experienced sexual abuse in childhood need to have immorality defined. As we deepen regularly, we become aware of the boundary enmeshment of others and of the subtle to blatant ways that we encourage boundary enmeshment.

> The people, therefore, must be set completely free from their old patterns of thought, that all their attention may be focused upon these new principles, for these are the light of this time and the very spirit of this age.[10]

> Now hath the Truth appeared, and falsehood fled away; now hath the day dawned and jubilation taken over, wherefore men's souls are sanctified, their spirits purged, their hearts rejoiced, their minds purified, their secret thoughts made wholesome, their consciences washed clean, their inmost selves made holy. . . .[11]

> There are certain pillars which have been established as the unshakable supports of the Faith of God. The mightiest of these is learning and the use of the mind, the expansion of consciousness, and insight into the realities of the universe and the hidden mysteries of Almighty God.''[12]

Let's look at what happens to us during the process of boundary enmeshment to find out why we may be unable to free ourselves from it. To review, the powers that make up authority of self are: The power of recognizing Him, power of discernment, the power of wisdom, limitations (boundaries), understanding, perception, identity, utterance, thought, reasoning, faith, imagination, inner vision, the affective power, the cognitive power, will, memory, discovery, reflection, intellectual investigation of truth, induction, and deduction. (See chapter 4.)

Much of the communication for a child exposed to trauma was one-way. As a child, having the opportunity to make the verbal expression of perceptions, to express one's identity or needs and feelings in consultation was not only unheard of, it was prohibited. If we used the power of speech to guard our identity, sexuality, or possessions, we most certainly would have been punished. An assertion of the power of will or choice that would allow one to set limits with others would have resulted in a punishment of some kind. The ability and right to explore truth out loud with the power of reason was thwarted. Inductive and deductive powers were used to escape threats rather than for resolution of problems. Imagination was not guided by nurturing adults to a mature separation of fantasy from creativity, or a helpful visualization of solutions and the development of art. The power of memory may not have been available to develop a concept of consequences, so we may have appeared to be irresponsible. And the use of the all-powerful word "no" was forbidden. We were disempowered by an authority which taught us we had no right to set boundaries. And we were forced to submit to boundary enmeshment.

The Use of Force

Being "forced" to do anything is a boundary violation and is not condoned in the writings of the Bahá'í Faith. In the following passage, the Báb alludes to the restraint God observes: "God desireth not to straiten the heart of anyone, be it even an ant, how much less the heart of a superior creature, except when he suffereth himself to be wrapt in veils, for God is the Creator of all things."[13] In a letter written on behalf of the Universal House of Justice to an individual believer, they state:

> The use of force by the physically strong against the weak, as a means of imposing one's will and fulfilling one's desires, is a flagrant transgression of the Bahá'í Teachings.

There can be no justification for anyone compelling another, through the use of force or through the threat of violence, to do that to which the other person is not inclined. 'Abdu'l-Bahá has written, "O ye lovers of God! In this, the cycle of Almighty God, violence and force, constraint and oppression, are one and all condemned." Let those who, driven by their passions or by their inability to exercise discipline in the control of their anger, might be tempted to inflict violence on another human being, be mindful of the condemnation of such disgraceful behavior by the Revelation of Bahá'u'lláh.[14]

O MY FRIENDS!
Walk ye in the ways of the good pleasure of the Friend, and know that His pleasure is in the pleasure of His creatures. That is: no man should enter the house of his friend save at his friend's pleasure, nor lay hands upon his treasures nor prefer his own will to his friend's, and in no wise seek an advantage over him. Ponder this, ye that have insight![15]

Being "forced" to do anything that would keep you from observing the Covenant of Bahá'u'lláh is also a boundary violation. Some obvious boundary violations would include verbal or physical sexual violations encompassing everything from subtle sexual suggestion to rape. Those who are spiritually developed feel revulsion when their lives are touched by this type of enmeshment and shrink back from it. The traumatized, however, having been dulled from their experiences, may not always recognize that internal alarm.

Internal Alarms

What are internal alarms? How can we recognize them? And why don't the traumatized act when an internal alarm sounds? Many traumatized people have been desensitized to signs of danger because they lived with it for so many years. As a result, they learned to ignore their internal alarm. Here are some internal alarms of which we may be unaware. We would classify these as *physical sensations:* muscle spasms in the chest or back, shallow breathing, fist or jaw clenched, mutilating of the fingers by picking the skin off, adrenalin rush, hands shaking, migraine headache, spastic colon, rapid heart beat, asthma, face flushed, nerve pain in the body, or being possessed by an extreme amount of physical energy or other sensations.

If you experience any of these physical sensations *chronically,* you may want to examine your relationships for boundary enmeshment. If you are being treated by your doctor on a regular basis for any of these physical sensations or conditions, looking to find a link between your daily stress reactions and boundary enmeshment is important.[16]

These sensations are your body's way of alerting you to boundary violations of which you need to become aware. Though you may not be conscious of it now, on a deeper level, your soul knows something is amiss. Unconscious memories of an early abuse pattern may be trying to surface.

Strong emotions which are unaccounted for can also be an internal alarm trying to create consciousness of danger, especially the feelings of resentment and revenge, irrational anger, the feeling that someone is trying to control you, the sense of being manipulated or taken advantage of, or suddenly being possessed by stubbornness, rigidity, or nervous laughter.

Even if we are conscious of our internal alarms, we may be reluctant to act on them and set a boundary because we are desperate to please (authoritarian training), because we are desperate to be accepted, or because we have an inordinate fear of authority. We certainly wouldn't have the skills to try, in any case.

No matter what reason prevents you from being aware of boundary enmeshment or violation at this stage, you do have many unconscious ways of protecting yourself when someone oversteps your boundaries. They are called *defense mechanisms.* Below is a brief discussion of many of the common ones.

Depression: Because you think you would hurt someone with your feelings of anger, you turn your anger inward and self-punish. You then experience depression, not connecting it to a boundary violation which occurred two hours ago. You are discounting your powers of reason, understanding, inner vision, perception, and faith. You internalize the messages, "Don't talk. Don't set boundaries. Don't make choices. Don't be different."

Repression: Since you don't have the verbal skills or ability to deal with the boundary violator, or because you sense danger, you may repress the knowledge of inappropriate behavior. The cognitive power is repressed.

Blocking the conflict out of your consciousness means you can avoid dealing with it. Yet the sad truth is that you'll have to keep facing the problem over and over again, since it never gets resolved. Blocked anxiety is *energy* which causes the physical sensations mentioned earlier. Energy released through taking appropriate action prevents physical discomfort, illness, and depression. You internalize the message, "Don't be aware."

Dissociation: If you space out, or go into a trance, you also avoid the conflict of confronting someone with their enmeshment in your life or your identity. You may stay in bed, preventing yourself from taking care of your daily routine, including the responsibilities you have to your employer, your family, and caring for your personal needs. You are repressing the powers of faith, volition, memory, reflection, identity, action, speech, and the affective power. You have internalized the messages, "Don't feel. Don't talk. Don't know yourself. Don't try. Don't think."

Isolation: By choosing to isolate, you withdraw from society in general, including other friends. This shows that trust is a strong issue with you. The powers of reasoning, faith, and identity need to be developed. You have internalized the message "Don't trust."

Minimization: You tell yourself the situation isn't so bad. You've known much worse. When you minimize, you numb your feelings, including your internal alarm. The affective power needs to be developed, as does the power of perception. You have internalized the messages, "Don't feel. Don't know yourself. Don't be afraid."

Rationalize: You say: "He/she was having a bad day. She was sick. He was drunk. She was tired. He couldn't help it; he was overstressed." Rationalizing means you don't hold them responsible for their behavior. Their behavior is OK because they were sick, drunk, tired. You may even rationalize that it was your fault, thus discounting your internal alarm. The powers of reasoning and speech need to be combined with the power of intellectual investigation of truth. You have internalized the messages, "Don't take care of yourself. Don't set boundaries. Don't disobey or challenge authority."

Denial: You may say: "I'm fine, really I am." Or: "It didn't really happen. She didn't really mean to hurt me. There isn't a problem." This denies your internal alarm. To overcome this, the powers of reasoning and speech need to be combined with the power of intellectual investigation of truth. You have internalized the messages, "Don't be afraid. Don't feel. Don't think. Don't learn and grow. Don't lead. Don't be smart or intelligent."

Rage: You may experience "irrational anger," exploding into a rage—at which point you will be embarrassed, resentful, but not know the cause or the source. The focus will then be upon you and the "transgression" you committed by "your" rage, instead of on that which caused it. Awareness of physical sensation needs to be developed, along with the power of memory, the power of reasoning, intellectual investigation of truth, induction, deduction and the power of discovery. You have internalized the messages, "Don't be aware. Don't set boundaries. Don't know yourself. Don't be. Don't take care of yourself. Don't make choices. Don't challenge the lie. Don't be angry."

ANGER AS A STUMBLING BLOCK TO RECOVERY

We all may be familiar with the phenomenon of "stuffing" and "exploding," the two major models that can be found in a single family unit for expressing anger. These are the prime indicators that tell us we do not know appropriate ways to express our powers and thus deal with our anger.

To compound the problem, the direct and covert message we received was "don't be honest with your feelings," and because this freedom of expression was thwarted, we spent much time in a revengeful, bitter silence. When we cannot verbally express our emotional state, and are even taught to dismiss, ignore, or discount our feelings, we suffer from loss of a clear, powerful identity.

I used to be a passive-aggressive person. I couldn't be honest with my anger. I stuffed it on the job for ten years, passively accepting extra work. Because authority of self was undeveloped, I did not make choices to resolve my anger and negotiate my needs. I was in unbearable physical pain much of the time and undergoing biofeedback training. I finally decided that I was going to try to negotiate with my employer for a more fair distribution of the work load. I wrote out a list of needs. I rehearsed what I was going to say over and over again. I made an appointment with him at his convenience. I was self-assured. I was prepared. At 10 o'clock that morning he called me into his office. I sat down with notes in hand, opened my mouth to speak and I exploded! I ranted and raved and yelled for 10 minutes. He opened his mouth to say something and I yelled, "No! Don't say anything. You are so persuasive, you will try to talk me out of this." Then I let loose again for five more minutes. After I finished, I said, "And now I'm going home!" He asked me, "Are you coming back tomorrow morning?" I yelled; no, screamed was more like it, "Yes!" Then I went home.

When my anger finally subsided, I was terror-stricken by the consequences of what I had done. I realized I was going to have to go back and face him again the next day. I couldn't eat supper. I couldn't sleep. The next day I dragged myself into work with my tail between my legs. My employer was standing at the end of the hallway at my office door. I walked slowly toward him and said very meekly, "I'm sorry I blew up at you yesterday." He said, "You have nothing to apologize for. You were just sharing your feelings."

It was the first time I had shown anger on the job in over ten years. I had raged at home at my children, at the dog, but never on the job. It was a moment of grace. And at that moment of grace and embarrassment a door also opened. The next week there was to be a workshop on how to express anger. I signed up for the three-hour course, not knowing that I was going to spend the next six years researching anger, writing about it, and teaching others to express their anger. What I include in this chapter is a culmination of that work.

In order to further develop authority of self, heal my relationships, and thereby transform myself, I had to understand the purpose of anger, what rage and irrational anger are, and what Bahá'u'lláh expected of me. In defining anger and irrational anger, there are solutions. In knowing my powers, there are even greater solutions.

This section does not pretend to meet all the needs or requirements of those who are violent with their anger. But it will attempt to educate those traumatized who are need-deprived, boundary enmeshed, and developmentally delayed. If it also helps those who tend to physical violence, it is because we all benefit from an expansion of consciousness which is a by-product of education, especially the spiritual education we receive from the writings of Bahá'u'lláh.

I recall reading: "We have forbidden you dissension and conflict in My Books, and My Scriptures, and My Scrolls, and My Tablets,"[17] and I wondered: If behavior which causes dissension and conflict is forbidden and we who have been traumatized have witnessed nothing but dissension and conflict, what else is there? How can we learn to resolve conflict and reduce dissension without reverting to passive, compliant behavior that has always served to increase anger and decrease self-worth?

Bahá'u'lláh also says,

> For the tongue is a smoldering fire, and excess of speech a deadly poison. Material fire consumeth the body, whereas the fire of the tongue devoureth both heart and soul. The force of the former lasteth but for a time, whilst the effects of the latter endureth a century.[18]

I have always been deeply disturbed about how my addiction to rage was hurting my children. Try as I might, my anger was out of control.

I believe there are several steps between the preverbal state many of the traumatized are in and obedience to the instruction "be thou angered at none."[19] A discussion of the purpose of anger and the definition of it can lead us to resolution.

McKay, Rogers, and McKay[20] teach us that anger helps to serve a very useful purpose. When we or others are under physical attack, or threat, or being oppressed, anger helps us mobilize and escape. Anger helps us become aware of the need to define ourselves and set more clearly defined boundaries that show others where they stop and we begin. And anger helps us overcome the fear of asserting our needs. It thus becomes an "internal alarm" that "something is not right" and we need to do something about it.

I have come to believe that when the Bahá'í writings talk about anger, they are referring to the inappropriate expression of anger, not anger as a feeling (an internal alarm) that can guide us into making conscious moral and behavioral choices. Anger expressed and acted out through vilification (i.e. emotional abuse), violence which includes physical abuse, and sexual abuse are all behaviors which can be condemned—and behaviors are different than feelings. A person who justifies her angry behavioral choices on the sole basis of her feelings is reasoning with her emotions, which is a cognitive distortion.

We also need to have an understanding of what is happening to a person who is experiencing irrational anger and expressing it in a violent manner. Irrational Anger is an unconscious behavioral response to situations in which you do not have the awareness (consciousness) to perceive or recognize that your basic human needs are not being met, or the verbal ability to ask to have those needs met because some of your powers are undeveloped or withheld.

This is how irrational anger can be identified:

Suddenly I hate the world. I feel anger not only at someone or something in particular, but at the whole world. I can't let go of my anger. I can't shake it because I don't know what's causing it. I let my anger spread to other people, even inanimate objects. I find myself getting angrier and angrier, striking out at whatever is in front of me. I feel confused! Things don't make sense. I feel disoriented or lost. I don't know what I need or want![21]

How is a noble human being reduced to such a state? Surely a human being, the highest value in creation, would be fully conscious most of the time and be capable of making moral choices rather than lost in this confused extreme.

Need fulfillment becomes the powerful humbler of those who rage. But how do we fulfill that of which we are not conscious, and once we become conscious, that of which we tremble in fear? For to rid ourselves of irrational anger, we must first know what it looks like, face that which we fear, and claim that which we lack, the crucial powers that will help us fulfill our basic human needs.

At a time when we, in all our potential, needed to be taught step-by-step how to identify and give meaning to our feelings, wants, and needs, we were instead shamed for wanting, needing, and feeling. Consequently, as adults, when we had a need, because we did not want to feel that internalized shame, our need remained unconscious; or if it was conscious, we could not interpret it. We may also have been threatened and punished when we had a need in childhood, making it dangerous to express our needs, wants, and feelings. This is the beginning of irrational anger; deprivation of the power of utterance or speech, the cognitive power, the affective power, and the power of anticipation (see chapter 6).

We can maintain our equilibrium if we are conscious enough (cognitive power) to monitor and address our mild irritation, annoyance, impatience, or resentment when these feelings come up. Unfortunately, the early shaming of our needs has laid the foundation for stuffing these derivatives of anger until we explode irrationally in uncontrolled violence and antisocial behavior.[22]

We were shamed with these messages for even feeling anger.[23] Also, we were led to believe that feeling anger internally or showing anger on the face was inherently bad, even if it was because of an injustice or oppression. We were also shamed by being told that feeling anger is immature, unmanly, unladylike, barbaric, illogical, useless, and childish. In reality, "behaving" in anger can be all of this in an adult; but it still needs to be recognized as a possible response to trauma or a result of the loss or nondevelopment of authority of self.

We were also shamed by tyrannical and oppressive figures for having needs with negative messages (e.g., "You are selfish, willful, immature, stubborn, impatient, lazy, slow, disrespectful, ungrateful, spoiled, greedy, complaining, rude and rebellious"). These messages shamed our power of volition, speech, and identity.

While it is important for our spiritual development as human beings to avoid these traits, they can be the result of rigid, controlling, or abusive parenting. Some parents, teachers, and employers have used these labels in a distorted way because of their own distorted perceptions. Many parents label their child for life (e.g., if a child did not share at the age of two, he or she is still thought of as "selfish and ungrateful" at the age of forty-five). It may be that not sharing at the age of two years was an early manifestation of boundaries and not "selfishness" at all. How the child's behavior is interpreted is dependent upon the belief system, values, and education of the parent. "Labeling" is one of the ten cognitive distortions mentioned earlier (see page 89).

These shaming messages and labels influenced us to repress our feelings of anger and our needs before we could identify, describe, and express them in an ongoing process of learning language and working our way through the natural developmental stages of childhood—a process that is supposed to be supported by our caregivers. Utilizing our powers to negotiate our needs helps us to catch up in the areas where we are developmentally delayed.

Shoghi Effendi says we have a sacred obligation to express our views in consultation. The Bahá'í writings empower us by granting us the power of utterance. It is just as sacred to have the right to express our needs without being threatened, to have the prerogatives 'Abdu'l-Bahá designates to each member of the family. 'Abdu'l-Bahá states:

> According to the teachings of Bahá'u'lláh the family, being a human unit, must be educated according to the rules of sanctity. All the virtues must be taught the family. The integrity of the family bond must be constantly considered, and the rights of the individual family members must not be transgressed. The rights of the son, the father, the mother—none of them must be transgressed, none of them must be arbitrary. Just as the son has certain obligations to his father, the father, likewise has certain obligations to his son. The mother, the sister and other members of the household must have their certain prerogatives. All these rights and prerogatives must be conserved, yet the unity of the family must be sustained.[24]

And one of the pioneers in family systems theory, Virginia Satir, offers the Five Freedoms, which empower the soul: (please note that the comments in parentheses are my own)

1. The freedom to see and hear (perceive) what is here and now, rather than what was, will be or should be. (The power of perception vs. denial.)
2. The freedom to think what one thinks rather than what one should think. (The powers of reasoning, reflection, and understanding vs. fantasy.)
3. The freedom to feel what one feels, rather than what one should feel. (The affective power vs. "should" statements and dissociation.)
4. The freedom to want (desire) and to choose what one wants, rather than what one should want. (The power of volition and utterance vs. passivity and rationalizing.)
5. And the freedom to imagine one's own self-actualization, rather than playing a rigid role or always playing it safe. (The powers of intellectual investigation of truth, identity, imagination, induction, and discovery.)[25]

These powers are replaced with defense mechanisms such as: depression, minimizing, rationalizing, and denial. They provide protective illusion until we find safety to see the truth and speak the truth of our needs. As long as we are not consciously aware of our needs and do not have the developmental skills to ask to have them met, we will continue unconsciously to defend our undeveloped selves with irrational anger instead of acting to fulfill our needs. The power of action is blocked.

Living in isolation, we can control our irrational anger or at least keep it from harming others. But being isolated is lonely and thwarts our development still more. Living in a unified community as Bahá'u'lláh desires and commands becomes a difficult task for the traumatized. Yet He calls those with irrational anger to unity as well. Unity is a great test for all Bahá'ís, but it's almost impossible for those of us who have been traumatized to fully grasp. We have constructed a fortress of defense around ourselves.

The way out of a fortress of defense is development of our powers of speech, identity, understanding, wisdom, induction, and our cognitive and affective powers. If the cognitive power is distorted, each distortion needs to be defined and understood for we can attribute varying degrees of our confusion and violence to them as well. We can liken Burns' ten cognitive distortions to ''idle fancies and vain imagination.'' Bahá'u'lláh confirms that they are prevalent throughout the world: ''Most of the people are enwrapped in fancy and idle imaginings: Where are the exponents of Thy certitude, O Assurance of the of the worlds?''[26]

COGNITIVE DISTORTIONS AS STUMBLING BLOCKS TO RECOVERY

Cognitive distortions not only hinder the healing process greatly, but also serve as hindrances to spiritual growth and understanding. On this topic, 'Abdu'l-Baha wrote to a youth:

> O spiritual youth! Praise thou God that thou hast found thy way into the Kingdom of Splendours, and has rent asunder the veil of vain imaginings, and that the core of the inner mystery hath been made known unto thee. This people, all of them, have pictured a god in the realm of the mind, and worship that image which they have made for themselves. And yet that image is comprehended, the human mind

being the comprehender thereof, and certainly the comprehender is greater than that which lieth in its grasp; for imagination is but the branch, while mind is the root; and certainly the root is greater than the branch. Consider then, how all the peoples of the world are bowing the knee to a fancy of their own contriving, how they have created a creator within their own minds, and they call it the Fashioner of all that is—whereas in truth it is but an illusion. Thus are the people worshipping only an error of perception.[27]

What we can glean from this passage is that cognitive distortions are "errors of perception." We create them in our minds. We call them "truth"; and we follow them to the bitter end, creating such circumstances as dissension, disunity, depression, divorce, and sometimes suicide.

These types of thought processes are so common that they are unquestioningly accepted by the mass of society. They are inherent in the mind of those who practice any form of prejudice against a person or group of people whom they perceive as inferior to themselves. They are also prevalent in the minds of those who perpetrate and justify all kinds of abuse, as well as those who cannot heal themselves from trauma.

To sanctify the mind and make it holy is to free ourselves from these "errors of perception," through the "spirit of enlightenment." We do this through reading the Bahá'í writings and placing new perception next to these errors of perception. Thus, again, we develop the power of discernment through seeing the contrast between the writings and the "idle words" on the tablet of the heart. Bahá'u'lláh speaks to all humanity in this Hidden Word, for He knows how humanity is prone to nurturing idle fancies:

O SON OF MAN!
The light hath shone on thee from the horizon of the sacred Mount and the spirit of enlightenment hath breathed in the Sinai of thy heart. Wherefore, free thyself from the veils of idle fancies and enter into my court, that thou mayest be fit for everlasting life and worthy to meet Me. Thus may death not come upon thee, neither weariness nor trouble.[28]

Here is a list of the most common cognitive distortions and how they contribute to the irrational anger of someone who has been traumatized or become boundary enmeshed:

Mental Filter: We may see current events through the filter of the past abuse that pervades our reality, actually believing that our overreaction is caused by the event in the present.

Labeling: Because we label ourselves as selfish, greedy, complaining, or willful when we have a need, we not only stuff our needs, we stuff our anger about not getting our needs met, until it emerges in irrational ways. We may also label the behavior of other people as selfish, greedy, complaining, or willful because they have needs.

Should Statements: We punish ourselves with "should" statements. We "should" not be selfish, greedy, complaining or willful, *nor should anyone else!* If our value system says our needs can't be met, then neither can anyone else's. This belief can serve as justification for rage, violent behavior, even as vandalism.

Jumping to Conclusions: We automatically assume someone is out to get us, means us harm, is going to punish us if we make a mistake, try to get our needs met, or express our feelings of anger—even though there are no definite facts that convincingly support our conclusion. This justifies our defending ourselves with irrational anger.

Over-Generalization: We generalize that authority "always" punishes, "never" understands, will "never" negotiate, "always" has a hidden agenda, and that "nothing" we try seems to work. And because we truly believe this, we automatically give up on our needs, only to continue stuffing them till we blow up again.

Emotional Reasoning: On the rare occasion when we become conscious of a need, try to set a boundary, or start to express our feelings of anger, fear, anxiety, shame, or confusion, we think: "If I'm feeling this 'bad,' I must be doing something wrong!" We then back down, withdraw, and give up on our needs, eventually reverting to irrational anger because our needs are never met.

Personalization: Because we learned to "please" others by being overly compliant, we assumed falsely that our compliant behavior could control the actions of others and thus make our environment a safer place. This means that if we did the "wrong" thing, we felt we were responsible for the abusive treatment that ensued. (It was my fault that she hit me. I got in the way.) This is the reason we personalize. We then accept the shame and blame authoritarian people lay at our feet. This not only creates depression, but is crazy-making and contributes to rage or irrational anger because nothing we try seems to work. We again give up on our needs. Pleasing others continues to be our greatest "conscious need."

All-or-Nothing Thinking: Because we want to escape shame and blame, we try even harder to perfect our ability to please others, setting ourselves up for failure since it's impossible to please everyone. Because we use perfection to control our environment in an effort to feel safe, we can't accept anything less than perfection. Our mental, emotional, and physical safety is again at stake. When we do fail, a scathing, internalized authoritarian voice shames and blames us as total failures. This voice is a remnant of the black-and-white system which we witnessed in childhood.

Disqualifying the Positive: The child within us remembers and parrots all the negative messages heard every time a failure occurred. We were taught to discount and contradict every good thing we achieved. We can't even count the fulfillment of a need as positive. We label it as selfish. Whatever perfection we achieve on the job or in our personal life is discounted, too.

Catastrophizing: We tell ourselves "bad" things are going to happen to us if we try to fulfill our needs. We imagine scenario after scenario of what other people's response to us is going to be, catastrophizing about being judged, imagining that "bad" things are going to happen to us if we ask to have a need met. Catastrophizing is founded on memories of abuse and punishment and pushes us to defend ourselves irrationally.

Magnification/Minimization: We minimize our needs and magnify the needs of others. We have been taught by authoritarianism to discount our own needs and focus on the needs of others. When we repeatedly minimize our needs, we become martyrs, eventually blowing up in irrational anger because our needs are "never" met (overgeneralization).[29]

If we can get over these ten *Cognitive Distortions,* we can have compassion for ourselves and others while we work out the solution using consultation.

The following nine thoughts are examples of how cognitive distortions that we express internally can block our ability to set boundaries and thereby to resolve our anger, keep ourselves safe, or be obedient to God's commandments. They show how our thinking is fraught with fear. Once they are externalized through the power of speech, we at least have the opportunity to confront them out loud:

1. **"He won't like me if I have needs or wants."**
   You are *catastrophizing* and *jumping to conclusions.*

2. **"She is going to get mad or I am going to hurt her feelings if I am honest about what I need."**
   You are *catastrophizing, jumping to conclusions, personalizing,* and implying that you are responsible if she explodes in anger when you set a boundary. You are also caretaking her feelings and needs exclusively, ignoring your own need for safety. Equality means both parties get their needs met.

3. **"What will people think of me if I do something so selfish?"**
You are imagining that others will attach a negative "label" to your behavior because you have a need for safety and a need to define your boundaries. You are also *over-generalizing*, thinking "all" people would think you are selfish. Some might, but not all.

4. **"I'm a terrible, selfish person to need or want this."**
You are *labeling* yourself in the same way the authoritarian person in your childhood did. You are also doing *emotional reasoning*: If you feel as if you are selfish to set a boundary or fulfill a need, you think it must be true. You are also *magnifying* your supposed fault and doing *all-or-nothing* thinking which states you must be totally unselfish and have no needs or rights of your own to be accepted by God, your friends, relatives or employer.

5. **"Maybe it's my fault."**
Needs and wants are not "faults." A physical and spiritual existence requires need-fulfillment and the setting of boundaries. Bahá'u'lláh revealed God's laws for the purpose of protecting the needs and rights of all. "He is the Protector of all in this world and the next."[30] By claiming responsibility, you are *personalizing* the other person's shame or blame, taking responsibility for his decision to enmesh himself in your boundaries. You are also not letting him own his own behavior. You are saying it's your fault if he beat you because you didn't shut up soon enough or read the writing on the wall fast enough or didn't guess the situation quick enough. You are owning his behavior.

6. **"Maybe if I were different this wouldn't have happened."**
You are *personalizing* again. Her boundary enmeshment is her responsibility because it is her behavior. You can be responsible only for your own behavior. You could be "different," and she would still become enmeshed in your boundaries or someone

else's because of her stage of development. Let her be responsible for her own behavior.

O YE SONS OF SPIRIT!
Ye are My treasury, for in you I have treasured the pearls of My mysteries and the gems of My knowledge. Guard them from the strangers amidst My servants and from the ungodly amongst My people.[31]

7. "What if I'm wrong and it turns out badly?"

You are *catastrophizing*. Being a Bahá'í doesn't mean you will never have to set boundaries and define yourself and your needs. Respect for boundaries by both parties will help us maintain unity in the community. Unity doesn't mean others don't have to know where they end and you begin. We are not supposed to allow others to tyrannize us. As the Bahá'í writings state:

> The friends of God must be adorned with the ornament of justice, equity, kindness and love. As they do not allow themselves to be the object of cruelty and transgression, in like manner they should not allow such tyranny to visit the handmaidens of God. He, verily, speaketh the truth and commandeth that which benefitteth His servants and handmaidens. He is the Protector of all in this world and the next.[32]

O OPPRESSORS ON EARTH!
Withdraw your hands from tyranny, for I have pledged Myself not to forgive any man's injustice. This is My covenant which I have irrevocably decreed in the preserved tablet and sealed with My seal.[33]

O REBELLIOUS ONES!
My forbearance hath emboldened you and My long-suffering hath made you negligent, in such wise that ye have spurred on the fiery charger of passion into perilous ways that lead unto destruction. Have ye thought Me heedless or that I was unaware?[34]

8. "I can't set a boundary or I would feel guilty. I should be more patient."

You are using *emotional reasoning*. If you feel guilty, you think it must be true. You are also using *should statements* to whip yourself as your authoritarian upbringing taught you to do. You think you "should" be able to endure tyranny. *Should statements* are also used to shame yourself. They lead right into *personalizing*, taking responsibility for the abuser's behavior. And you are *labeling* yourself as impatient.

Taking a risk to share your needs, wants, and feelings means you set a boundary instead of reverting to unconscious behavior, i.e., irrational anger, defense mechanisms, revenge, or constant internal resentment. These are what cause conflict, dissension, and disunity. Honest sharing means needs, wants, and feelings can be part of consultation to resolve boundary enmeshment. As Bahá'u'lláh states:

O MY FRIENDS!
Walk ye in the ways of the good pleasure of the Friend, and know that His pleasure is in the pleasure of His creatures. That is: no man should enter the house of his friend save at the friend's pleasure, nor lay hands upon his treasures nor prefer his own will to his friend's, and in no wise seek an advantage over him. Ponder this, ye that have insight.[35]

9. "I choose/choose not to set a boundary."

Congratulations. You've just taken control and accepted authority of self. Otherwise you would have said, "I *can't* set a boundary." As long as you know that you are making a choice, authority over your own decisions rests in your own hands.

When I encounter the traumatized, I have often refrained from setting boundaries with them because they are initially boundaryless. First I create awareness for them of their own boundaries and teach them the language of how to set boundaries; then I thoroughly ground them in this self-protective process by calling their attention to differences between us.

I demonstrate further by establishing boundaries with them—

all the while creating safety, reassuring them, and acknowledging their nobility.

Think of it this way: I cannot expand my boundaries indefinitely, or I would lose my psychological and spiritual balance. But I will purposely expand my boundaries temporarily in order to create a point of safety and unity with others. Once unity and safety are achieved, I will then need to secure my boundaries once more in order to recreate balance in my life. I will need time to fulfill the needs of self which I have set aside out of a strong desire to nurture others. By this process of observing me alternately expanding and securing my boundaries, the traumatized can be taught how to expand and secure their own boundaries and fulfill their own needs.

Read through this chapter often to identify the pitfalls that usually prevent you from setting boundaries with others. It will prepare you to identify your internal alarms, including physical sensations and feelings, help you to become conscious of and set aside your defense mechanisms, and to recognize and discard your cognitive distortions.

You will understand more fully that they are a response to trauma and realize there is no reason to shame yourself because you use them; but there is a need to become conscious of them in order to eliminate unnecessary and ineffective thoughts and to enable yourself to make conscious moral and behavioral choices.

When you are able to define this much of you to yourself, you will be able to confidently define yourself to another human being in consultation. You will feel strong when you clearly define yourself. Others can't know who you are if you continue hiding behind your defense mechanisms. And you can't begin to know your potential to exercise authority of self if your thinking is clouded by cognitive distortions.

Once you have all this information, you can begin to take the risk of telling others what you need, want, and feel so that they will know what boundaries are specific to you as an individual. Others may feel strong, uncomfortable feelings because your honest risk is a challenge to their belief system. As you grow in awareness and share your awareness with others, it will help them to grow also.

Chapter 6

Aiding the Traumatized: How Communities and Individuals Can Help

Introduction

This chapter offers suggestions and tools for individuals, communities, and local Spiritual Assemblies dealing with those who have been traumatized. It describes the issues with which you will be confronted when acting as a mediator for those who may be confused, depressed, fearful, or acting out in self-destructive or other-destructive ways. First, there are clear-cut instructions on how to direct the traumatized to the safety of therapy. There is also an examination of the major blocks to the consultation process, a list of stumbling blocks that interfere with consultation, plus methods to facilitate consultation. The chapter continues with a discussion of suicide prevention, domestic abuse, listening to the traumatized, and creating protective behaviors to avoid abuse and trauma. This information is not meant to replace therapy or counseling, but only as a guide to identifying issues with which you may be confronted.

The Bahá'í Faith: A Safe Harbor

The Bahá'í Faith attracts people in various stages of need, some of whom are desperately seeking safety and solace. By its very nature, the Bahá'í Faith is a safe harbor not only for those who have been oppressed politically, racially, religiously, economically, and because of gender in a system that believes women to be inferior; but it is also a refuge for men and women who have experienced the trauma of being raised in a tyrannical system of child rearing. All these are bringing a hesitant trust to Bahá'u'-lláh.

Those who have lost their faith in a just God because of their trauma are turning toward the Bahá'í Faith to learn what Bahá'u'lláh's Revelation has to say about God's compassion and mercy. Many may have ceased to plead in prayer and to lament their sorrow to the God they may feel has betrayed His Covenant to them, if they have ever heard of God's Covenant. They feel terribly alone in their private world, beaten down by so much suffering and loss before a seemingly silent God. They ask, "Where was God's divine, all-encompassing mercy for me?"

Hypervigilant against an unknown or projected threat, they isolate themselves from others, afraid to trust even for a moment and afraid to let their vigilance fail lest trust be dashed again. No wonder Bahá'u'lláh said, "The vitality of men's belief in God is dying out in every land; nothing short of His wholesome medicine can ever restore it."[1]

By translating the words of Bahá'u'lláh into deeds, Bahá'ís, whether through their institutions such as the Local Spiritual Assembly or an individual member of the community, will create a healing community in which trust can be restored. We are guided in this process with clear teachings from 'Abdu'l-Bahá.

> God has created all, and all return to God. Therefore, love humanity with all your heart and soul. If you meet a poor man, assist him; if you see the sick, heal him; reassure the affrighted one, render the cowardly noble and courageous, educate the ignorant, associate with the stranger. Emulate God. Consider how kindly, how lovingly He deals with all, and follow His example. You must treat people in accordance with the divine precepts—in other words, treat them as kindly as God treats them, for this is the greatest attainment possible for the world of humanity.[2]

No soul should be hated, none neglected; nay, rather, their very imperfections should demand greater kindness and tender compassion.[3]

This sounds very sympathetic, but our sympathy alone will not heal the traumatized. They also need to be encouraged to learn how to meet their own needs, to be responsible, respectful, cooperative human beings able to enter into community life. They need to develop the components of authority of self so they will be able to make healthy changes in their own lives, rather than have changes always imposed by external forces. Ian Semple states,

> It is true that Bahá'ís need to have loving understanding for *all* their fellow human beings, no matter how depraved their actions. For example, in 'Abdu'l-Bahá's prayer from the Tablet revealed to the Bahá'ís of the United States and Canada, which begins 'O God, my God! Thou seest how black darkness is enshrouding all regions . . .', having described the atrocities committed by the feuding peoples, He says 'O Lord! Have pity on these ignorant ones, and look upon them with the eye of forgiveness and pardon . . .' Nevertheless, there are clear statements in the Writings that certain kinds of behavior *are* bad and unacceptable, and Bahá'u'lláh even prescribes punishments for some of them. Moreover, there is very definite authority which Spiritual Assemblies are expected to exert and the authority of parents over their children.[4]

Those who have responded destructively to their trauma may feel a great deal of shame and guilt. It must be stressed that we cannot completely assuage the anguish of their guilt lest the standards of morality be relaxed.

> I fully agree that the feeling of obligation, like any virtue, can be carried to an extreme. One has to learn to accept one's own imperfection and recognize that it is the human condition that one continually fails and must just pick oneself up and try again. But I think that it is the relaxation

of standards of morality—the spread of the idea that each person should be entirely free to express himself or herself, no matter what, that is one of the major contributing factors in the mental, physical, and sexual abuse of other people. There are certain acts in respect to which a person should be trained to feel a profound revulsion, and hence a deep shame if he or she commits them. Jesus implies this in relation, for example, to the ill-treatment of children:

> But whoso shall offend one of these little ones which believe in me, it were better for him that a millstone were hanged about his neck, and that he were drowned in the depth of the sea.[5]

Ian Semple continues,

> Of course, I recognize that one should not stress this aspect of things when dealing with a traumatized person, because he or she has suffered from an excess of authority; but I think it is important not to generalize the concept so that the impression is given that it is not good to feel guilty over a dereliction of duty. . . .
>
> One thought occurred to me, which you do not mention, and I wondered if this would be helpful in dealing with traumatized people. This is in relation to their tendency to feel that they themselves must be "bad" because of what happened to them. There is a clear distinction in Bahá'í thought between the character of a deed as it relates to the perpetrator and the sufferer of it. The extreme example is martyrdom. The murderer of a martyr commits a heinous offense, and in relation to him his deed is a crime. Although the deed is the same deed it becomes, in relation to the martyr, the greatest blessing that he can receive. Now this is clearly far from being entirely analogous to other abuses of one person by another. Nevertheless it makes the point that participation in a repulsive act by the person against whom the act is perpetrated has a fundamentally different character from that of the participation of the perpetrator.[6]

'Abdu'l-Bahá speaks of "educating" those who are ignorant. Its root word is "educaré," which means to draw out from within what is already there, rather than to impose upon from the outside. Some of the knowledge of how to solve their problems is embedded in the life experience of the traumatized. This has provided at once a terrible and a practical education. If we as individuals can tap into the many practical and irrational ways they have learned to survive in a hostile world, they will learn how many answers actually come from within and how "intact" instead of "dysfunctional" they really are. The traumatized are more developmentally delayed and disempowered than dysfunctional, a word currently being used. The truth is they have learned to "function" in an extremely dysfunctional setting. When our dependency needs are not met in childhood, we are said to be developmentally delayed. We appear to be adult, yet our feelings, cognitive ability, and volition may be those of a child. We are developmentally disempowered when others determine our role in life, our identity, or prevent us from questioning and conducting an independent search for truth.

Counseling: What to Do, Where to Go, and Whom to Call

Chapter 1 was an illustration of how early life situations can result in chronic distress that is very confusing to those who experience it. It can also lead them to the conclusion that life is not worth living. Those who are experiencing chronic distress need to be referred to the professional healing community. In a letter written on behalf of the Guardian, the importance of this is stressed,

> Healing through purely spiritual forces is undoubtedly as inadequate as that which materialist physicians and thinkers vainly seek to obtain by resorting entirely to mechanical devices and methods. The best result can be obtained by combining the two processes: spiritual and physical.[7]

Depression, fantasies, anxiety attacks, phobias, and flashbacks distort reality for the traumatized. They need to be strongly advised to get into counseling with someone who can help them sort out their feelings, their thoughts, memories, experiences, and behavior, especially if all of these components of their reality are distorted. If they're consumed with fear and shame, they will have to find out what the fear and shame is about. If they're consumed with rage, they will have to uncover what is triggering the rage. Their emotions may be way out of proportion to the issues to which they are responding.

If they're not able to respond to the present clearly, they need some objective person to be a strong sounding board for them. If they are depressed, they will need medical attention as well as psychological guidance. The goal of counseling and therapy is to get people functioning if they're not. Some who are seriously traumatized will have to be hospitalized or institutionalized. Others may need only brief therapy that doesn't deal with past issues. The approach for brief therapy is: It doesn't matter what is causing the difficulty. This is what you can do to get rid of it. People who have long term therapy, from 1 to 2 years, report the greatest benefit for firmly entrenched patterns of depression and behavior.[8]

As the Guardian notes in a letter written on his behalf to an individual believer:

> You must always remember, no matter how much you or others may be afflicted with mental troubles and the crushing environment of these State Institutions, that your spirit is healthy, near to our Beloved, and will in the next world enjoy a happy and normal state of soul. Let us hope in the meantime scientists will find better and permanent cures for the mentally afflicted. But in this world such illness is truly a heavy burden to bear![9]

And further:

> There are a great many as you know mental diseases and troubles at present, and the one thing Bahá'ís must not do is take a defeatist attitude toward them. The power in the Faith is such that it can sustain us on a much higher level in spite of whatever our ailments might be than other people who are denied it. This however does not mean that we should

ignore medical opinion and treatment. On the contrary, we should do our best to procure the opinion of specialists and competent doctors.[10]

What to Do

A first step is to contact their family physician, the Local Spiritual Assembly, a relative, or a close friend to alert them that there is a problem. These professionals, relatives, and friends may have prior knowledge and past experiences with the individual who is under stress and therefore can offer assistance. Find out who or what they might recommend for counseling. The traumatized may trust the recommendations of a good friend who has had a satisfactory experience with a therapist.

In any event, finding a therapist is a very personal thing. The important part will be the relationship between the therapist and the client. The client will have to feel there is compatibility for not only the issues they need to explore but for the personalities that will be working together as well. Another important point is to have the client involved in the choice process. Encourage them to work until they find the right person for themselves. It is also important to follow up to make sure they are staying on task. "In the Bahá'í Teachings it is made quite clear that when one is ill, one should seek the best available medical advice. This naturally leaves a person free to choose what they consider good in medical opinion."[11]

Bear in mind that "asserting" oneself to get therapy requires individualist qualities. Someone who is more of a collectivist will worry about taking money and time away from their family, even though they are desperately in need of counseling. They may even shame themselves internally because this is a "selfish" act. These two concepts may have to be explained to the traumatized individuals so they understand that Bahá'u'lláh's Revelation integrates the best of both individualism and collectivism, while warning us to avoid extremes of either—i.e., the rights and prerogatives of the individual must not be arbitrarily pursued, yet the unity of the family must be maintained. Also, Bahá'u'lláh indicates in these quotations that the care of self can be integrated with the care of others:

O MY SERVANTS!
Ye are the trees of My garden; ye must give forth goodly and
wondrous fruits, that ye yourselves and others may profit
therefrom.[12]

O MY SERVANT!
The best of men are they that earn a livelihood by their
calling and spend upon themselves and upon their kindred
for the love of God, the Lord of all worlds.[13]

Where to Go

There are a number of government and private services that are
available in most communities that can assist Assemblies (see fig.
6.1. on page 121). Be sure to contact as many of the agencies as
may apply to the situation that presents itself to the Assembly.

Whom to Call

There are a variety of disciplines that offer counseling. Social
workers who are MSWs (Masters of Social Work) and psychiatric
nurses with private practices are favored by some of today's
budget-minded insurers, because they offer services that are far
lower in cost than a psychiatrist or Clinical Psychologist. Marriage and Family therapists are also available, as are therapists
who specialize in multiple personality disorder and cult abuse.
Family Violence shelters are available in most cities. A therapist
who knows women's issues (usually a woman) can be especially
helpful to someone who is being battered. A psychologist who
specializes in helping those who have been sexually abused is
essential for those who have experienced that type of abuse.
There are specialists for overeaters and those who are anorexic or
bulimic, as well as support groups for every type of abuse just
mentioned. Most newspapers publish a weekly schedule of support groups in the area. Clip it out and have the secretary of the
Local Spiritual Assembly keep it in a folder for ready use.

The type of professional that is chosen to assist may depend
upon the availability of funds. Ask the professional questions
about who can provide services to the indigent if necessary.
Also, check your telephone directory under social services to
find out whether there are services for those who can't afford the
cost of therapy. Find out whether the believer needs transporta-

Where to go for assistance

Public Aid	Police Departments
Department of Children and Family Services	Independent Medical Practitioners
Child Abuse Hotline	Marriage and Family Counselors
Suicide Hotline	School Counselors
County Health Department	Department of Rehabilitation
Human Resources Department	Public Housing Department
Social Service Organizations	The Public Library for free resources
Community Centers	Alcoholics Anonymous
Women's Organizations	Alanon
YWCA	Big Brothers/Big Sisters
Family Violence Shelters	Narcotics Anonymous
Legal Aid Services	Survivors of Incest Anonymous

Fig. 6.1. A listing of some government and private agencies, organizations, and groups to go to for assistance.

tion to and from therapy or the services of a baby sitter. Create a mentoring program for children whose needs are going unmet because their caregiver is mentally ill. Most directors of family violence shelters have a nationwide directory on hand to tell you how to contact shelters in other cities if necessary.

If an Assembly is dealing with a legal matter, it should be cognizant of the following guidance offered by the Universal House of Justice:

> Your Assembly should make a distinction between those actions which can be dealt with at present by the Bahá'í administrative institutions and those which are criminal in character and fall within the purview of the civil authorities. In general, misconduct on the part of individual Bahá'ís and differences between the friends should be adjudicated by Spiritual Assemblies, and the friends should obey the Assemblies' decisions. However, in criminal matters in which the state claims a prior interest and has clearly laid down the procedures to be followed, and the action of Assemblies would amount to interference with these procedures, such matters must be referred to the civil authorities.
>
> Since at the present time Bahá'í institutions are not authorized to deal with criminal matters, you should seek the advice of legal experts in reconciling the observance of confidentiality, which is essential to the functioning of any Spiritual Assembly, and the Assembly's obligation to uphold Government regulations in criminal cases.[14]

What Would the Traumatized Hope to Get Out of Therapy?

With therapy, the traumatized would be able to live their lives more fully without past abuse constraining them. They would be able to get rid of the shame and secrets that motivate unconscious self-limiting and self-destructive behavior. Some would develop a stronger self-concept. This would lead to positive posture changes for some and the ability to achieve eye contact. They might achieve more self-acceptance and respect and acceptance of others, too.

A reduction in anger and rage is another positive outcome of therapy, as is being able to negotiate their needs and wants with others, perhaps for the first time. Therapy does not bestow "happiness" per se. But getting rid of the trauma and all of its self-limiting baggage can allow them to find significance and meaning in their lives. It is also hoped that relationships will work better, and they will be more satisfied with their life work. Some may be empowered to make a change of careers to achieve greater satisfaction.

In the long run, the lifetime spiritual and psychological quest for an individual Bahá'í seeking therapy would be to achieve unity of identity—a wholeness that would encompass having all the component parts of one's identity integrated with the Covenant of Bahá'u'lláh. (See p. 82.)

A conflict of values can be more correctly translated into a conflict of identity. Our behavior conflicts with our beliefs; our beliefs conflict with our feelings; our desires conflict with our speech; our fantasies conflict with the principles of the Bahá'í Faith; and our desire to be more individualistic conflicts with collectivist leanings. The traumatized are truly in a crisis of identity, a conflict of identity because they didn't have a stabilizing code of moral values while growing up. This is at the heart of some forms of mental illness. In the end, each of us is responsible for our behavior and for becoming obedient to God, regardless of what happened to us in our childhood.

Consultation with the Traumatized
The traumatized may be reluctant or unable to enter fully into honest consultation. Confusion may result because they are afraid to speak the truth. Remember there is always time; and their development or recovery does not have a timetable.

Compare the ideal qualities given to us by 'Abdu'l-Bahá for consultation with the stumbling blocks to consultation which face those who were traumatized (see figures 6.2 and 6.3 on pp. 124–125).

These blocks to reality and consultation are pretty much standard throughout literature on psychology.

Listening to the Traumatized Soul
In chapter 4, the powers of humankind were identified and defined. Here are four more qualities, or powers, that a listener

Ideal Qualities for Consultation	
The ability to express opinions and arguments with absolute freedom	Honesty of purpose
Humble fellowship	Frank discussion/candor
"humility and lowliness amongst His loved ones"	High sense of justice and duty
Modesty	Devotion to the welfare and interest of others
Open-mindedness	Harmony
Sincerity	Radiance of spirit
Detachment from all else save God	Servitude to His exalted threshold
Patience and long-suffering in difficulties	

Fig. 6.2. Ideal qualities for consultation

should strive to possess, that can aid in listening and responding to the traumatized soul. Being conscious of these qualities can help us understand what makes a good listener and how to be more attentive to his or her needs. It can be readily seen how they apply to both the listener and the speaker, and how the misuse of or failure to listen properly can perpetuate confusion and trauma.

The *power of anticipation or expectation:* This is the faculty that includes intuitive preconception, precognition, and presentiment. We can mentally and spiritually await the mercy and presence of our Lord—as in the introduction to the long obligatory prayer[15]—and know that our soul will be stirred in "response." On the negative side this power can include the

Stumbling Blocks to Consultation	

Unchallenged Defense Mechanisms such as:
• Dissociation (spacing out)
• Irrational anger
• Withdrawal/isolation
• Minimization (things aren't that bad)
• Rationalization (it happened because she was sick or tired)
• Denial (this hides needs, wants and feelings)
• Externalization (it's everyone else's problem)
	A personal belief system that says:
	  It is never safe to share feelings, ideas, opinions, needs or wants with authority figures because of these rules:
	
	  Don't talk!
	  Don't trust!
	  Don't think!
	  Don't feel!
	  Don't need!
	  Don't want!
	  Don't ask questions!

Displaced anger: Giving the heat of anger to others instead of connecting it to the abuser and past events	Role playing (not being authentic or congruent)
Controlling behavior	Manipulative behavior
Depression	Repression
Grandiosity	Illusions
Hyper-vigilance	Low self-worth
Transference: Believes and acts as if you are the disapproving parent	Need to be absolutely right

Fig 6.3. Stumbling blocks to consultation for those who were traumatized

formation of opinions before examining the evidence—in other words, prejudice. This applies to our prejudices of race, religion, class, and even homosexuality.[16]

The *power of receptivity* means being capable of taking in both the "knowledge of God" and entering (or receiving) the reality of another. We can be receptive to joy and peace; however, because of the fact that receptivity is a power that is affected by attitude, we can also be receptive to negative emotions and energy fields. We can assist the traumatized by helping them eliminate their blocks to unity or oneness. Some things that block our power of receptivity are preconceptions, predetermination, conditioning, our roles, our cultural heritage, and the negative use of the power of anticipation (manifested as prejudice, cynicism, doubt, and incredulity). Thus the power of faith supports our power of receptivity. The following quote of Bahá'u'lláh illustrates the importance of receptivity,

> Beseech God to grant unto men hearing ears, and sharp sight, and dilated breasts, and receptive hearts, that haply His servants may attain unto their hearts' Desire, and set their faces towards their Beloved.[17]

The *power of response* is a power that "answers" through physical, emotional, or mental action to a stimulus, influence, or principle that has been received. It is also called the power of execution by the Universal House of Justice, "Hence, at the very crux of any progress to be made is the individual believer, who possesses the power of execution which only he can release through his own initiative and sustained action."[18] When the response is one of joy, acceptance, justice, or mercy, it becomes a renewal of the soul. When the response is cruelty, vengeance, or alienation, it engenders remoteness from God. To be responseless is to give no reply, no answer to the reality of another who may be longing for a response. The power of response is the capacity to fulfill a trust, a need, or an obligation.[19]

The *power of attention* is a faculty of assiduously applying one's mind and observant powers in the service of those who are in need, in obedience to an authoritative summons. It is a state of being alert to every aspect of their situation, of learning humbly about it as it unfolds, remaining ever open to discover a possible action appropriate to their reality that could bring to an end the instability and turbulence caused by their trauma.[20]

We can help the traumatized recognize the connection between their fragmentation and their instability. The act of going from fragmentation to oneness or wholeness is an ordering of perception.[21]

Entering the Reality of Another

Entering the reality of another in an intimate situation is listening in a way that confirms the view of the other by treating their reality as sacred. This is what creates relationship. To do otherwise would be to deny their existence, their life experience, and disconfirm their reality of their self. If someone denied your life experience, it would tend to make you feel "crazy." We must not fear that confirming or acknowledging another's reality would be condoning of their behavior.

We can confirm or acknowledge the other by paraphrasing what they've said. However, if our response is tempered by judgment, interpretation, fixing, evaluating, or cross-examining,[22] we face the potential for making the traumatized feel defensive or in a one-down position. These styles can induce arguments, because they delay the ability of the traumatized to become conscious of their reality. Further, if I allow others to give me advice, fix me, convert me, or interpret my words for me, I abdicate my powers and perpetuate the disempowerment that was begun when I was a child. I also participate in an injustice toward myself, because these styles of response toward me do not allow me to see with my own eyes or hear with my own ears. These are the ways authority has sought to disempower me. These are the innocuous and covert ways that I have been forced to think with another's reality rather than becoming conscious of my own. This is boundary enmeshment.

These styles of response are the result of our own fragmentary awareness as assisters; and we have to own that. What we are looking for in paraphrasing is a response that lifts up to their power of attention the contents of their consciousness at this moment in time so it can be examined. It's a sustained openness/receptivity to the present when listening to another, a focusing on them. Banville says that the purpose of paraphrasing is to determine whether what we hear is what the speaker intended for us to hear: and it does this for the speaker's benefit, so that their reality is clarified, i.e., brought into awareness.

Here is an example: " 'I can't leave my husband,' she said, with a worried look on her face, 'because he has threatened to kill me if I leave. It's only when I say the wrong thing that he hits me.' Her hands shook as she reached for a glass of water."

This tells you that the speaker's life is in danger and that she is owning responsibility for his wrongdoing, blaming herself. The emotions you are witnessing are her worry and fear. The volitional aspect of her consciousness tells you that she has made the decision that she cannot leave. To paraphrase this we would pull it all together in this way: "It sounds like you are blaming yourself when your husband hits you. Am I reading you right?" (Pause for an answer.) "And you look worried and fearful because you have decided to stay. Are you worried?" You are lifting into her attention the content of what she has said, her emotions, and her choices. This is her reality as she has presented it to you. Once this has been confirmed, you can proceed further. The point is to help her clarify her reality, not to be a therapist.

Other phrases that are helpful are: "It sounds like you are thinking of hurting yourself. Are you?" "It sounds like you feel cynical that she will ever change. Do you?" "I hear you saying that you feel so hopeless that you want to run away. Am I hearing you correctly?" You put their feelings into words so that you can reflect them back to the speaker. You can do the same with the content and the decisions that are inferred in what they are saying.

We must listen with the discerning reality of the Bahá'í writings, not in judgment of the traumatized. The reality that includes a compassionate understanding of all of humanity progressing along a continuum of imperfection toward perfection is a healing one. Another purpose is to eventually (not at first by any means, but in good time) inform them of how the principles relate to their particular needs. The principles inform us of our rights: our right to safety, dignity, protection, and boundaries.

For example, a woman who is being battered doubts her own

worth and the worth of women in general. When we utilize the principle of the equality of men and women in the process of assistance, we have certitude in how to proceed, and this precious knowledge causes the confidence of the traumatized to increase. She has latent inner knowledge; confirmation of her powers through the sacred principles can make that knowledge conscious and free her power. Intellect, feelings, physical reactions—all must be conscious in order to tap into that which is within that can help the process of healing: her intuition or inner vision.

It is not by accident that 'Abdu'l-Bahá tells us to pray: "Manifest and make evident the signs of Thy oneness which have been deposited in all the realities of life. Reveal and unfold the virtues which Thou hast made latent and concealed in these human realities."[23] It is "oneness" that motivates us to relieve the oppression of the traumatized. If they are to find their way through the maze of self-destructive and other-destructive behavior, then their virtues—the powers that lie latent within their reality—must be released. Further, He teaches us to pray, "O Lord, help Thou Thy loved ones to . . . unravel the secrets that are treasured up in the inmost reality of all created beings. Make them to hear the hidden truths that are written and embedded in the heart of all that is."[24] The souls of the traumatized are shrouded in sad truths and dark secrets that need to be exposed to the light of Bahá'u'lláh's Revelation. We must be ready listeners to the secrets they share and, as these secrets are unraveled, the bitterness and anger that keeps their wounds festering will find release.

Listening and offering compassion does not imply that there are no boundaries in the oneness that we share. It is certainly true that some may be entering into community for the first time. This will exact patience from us in setting boundaries that are flexible while maintaining an individuality that supports their ability to recognize, perhaps for the first time in their life, that boundaries are necessary for their healing. Boundaries protect oneness, boundaries protect stability, and boundaries create consciousness of the commandments of God. The reverse is true, also. Oneness calls for boundaries to be respected, observed, and reciprocated; stability and tranquility help us to be thankful for boundaries; and the commandments of God help all of humanity to understand their limitations and boundaries. Reviewing chapter 5 can facilitate an understanding that it is the need to obey the commandments of God and execute the principles of Bahá'u'lláh that creates the necessity that both the assister and the traumatized set boundaries with each other. If the assister cannot or does not know how to set boundaries, he or she will lose their psychological and spiritual balance.

Suicide Prevention
Some of the traumatized who are suicidal are mentally ill; others are not. If you counsel them that this is a test and an opportunity to grow, you will be grossly ignoring and discounting the seriousness of their illness or the trauma they have endured. It is authoritarian to ignore the great emotional and mental needs and focus only on the rules and commandments of God.

We as individuals or members of Local Spiritual Assemblies can try to be less self-righteous, less moralizing, and more loving and understanding.

People attempt suicide for a variety of reasons. Sometimes it is because of the loss of a relationship. Sometimes it is because life has lost its meaning. Sometimes it is due to a physical ailment or loss of social or financial status. They may no longer value their life, or they may experience a sense of failure in meeting the standards expected by society. They may think of the world as a hostile place to live, or feel alienated and disconnected from community, family, and friends. The inability to adjust to social changes causes some to attempt suicide. Economic distress, an abrupt loss of meaningful supports and attachments, and the sorrow at holidays experienced by people from broken families are other possible causes. Finally, the traumatized may attempt suicide because of a family history of cruelty, violence, rejection, and abandonment.

Determining Who the Suicidal Are
Firstly, you need to determine whether the person is suicidal. The most direct way to do this is simply to ask them whether they are having thoughts about harming themselves. If they say no and you still think they may be contemplating suicide, watch for verbal, emotional, or behavioral distress signals:

- Direct statements like "I can't take it. I don't want to live anymore. I'm going to kill myself."

- Veiled and disguised clues. "Soon this pain will be over. They'll be sorry when I'm gone. No one cares about me. No one would miss me anyway."

- Other emotional clues. Rabbi Earl Grollman lists these:

> Any sudden change in a person's personality is always a perilous warning. Depression and despondency, imagining that they suffer from cancer, a lot of thoughts about death and dying, loss of appetite or sudden overeating, insomnia or excessive sleeping, unusual neglect of personal appearance, constant complaints about physical symptoms, persistent feelings of loneliness, worthlessness, feelings of sinfulness, guilt or sadness, ordinary tasks become difficult to perform, withdrawal and isolation from friends and family, decline in the quality of work, a lack of planning for the future—"Why worry about it? I could be dead tomorrow,"—and abrupt outbursts of anger, "jumping" at little things.
>
> Behavioral hints include: Beginning to drink or do drugs more frequently, giving away treasured or favorite items, and disappearing without telling anyone.[25]

Rabbi Grollman also says we must beware of oversimplification or jumping to conclusions, but we must be aware that a combination of distress signals manifested over time bears watching.

Many times those who are suicidal are ambivalent about actually dying—but they are emphatic about wanting to stop the immense pain they are in! You will *add* to their pain if you:

1. Tell them they shouldn't feel that way.
2. Tell them this is a test from God.
3. Tell them suicide is a "sin." Self-destruction is not a theological issue; it is the result of unbearable emotional stress.

4. Say: "Don't worry. Everything will be all right."
5. Say: "Think how much better off you are than others. You should be grateful."
6. Say: "Do you realize the pain and embarrassment you will cause your family?"
7. Say: "You don't really mean that."

How You Can Help the Suicidal Person

1. Recognize the clues of suicide listed above.
2. Believe the person with whom you are consulting, and act on your own judgment.
3. Form a nonjudgmental relationship, not only of words but of nonverbal empathy.
4. Be a good listener. Say: "It takes a lot of courage to share your feelings, and I appreciate your honesty."
5. Don't argue. You may lose not only the argument but also the individual.
6. Don't give false reassurance. They may well be driven to self-destruction by platitudes when they desperately need a concerned and honest response.
7. Suggest positive approaches. Try to discover what is still meaningful to them and who are those persons who still touch their life.
8. Dare to hope. When hidden thoughts emerge and are expressed with feelings, troubles may seem less complicated and more solvable. Ask them, "What changes can you make?" "What pressures can you say no to?" "Is there anyone you can turn to?"
9. Evaluate the seriousness of the suicide risk. The more specific they are in describing how they will do it, the greater the risk.
10. Don't leave the suicidal person alone in a high-risk situation. Stay with the person until the crisis passes or until help arrives. Relationships carry responsibility.
11. Get help. Try to connect with a competent professional.
12. The importance of continuing care and concern cannot be overstated.[26]

Protective Behaviors: What Can We Learn from Experience?

Sometimes we need to shake ourselves into awareness of danger, especially if we are raising children. We need to teach children good boundaries so that they will not be vulnerable to the unexpected encounter with a perpetrator of sexual abuse. We need to know for ourselves that there are measures that can be taken to fend off harm in order to endow our children with power to live in a world where trust must be earned. And while we must not catastrophize, we still need to be realistic. We cannot teach our children the fantasy that this is a safe world. Many of us have led sheltered lives, and this true story, which was related to me at the Bahá'í World Congress, serves as a warning that we cannot relax our boundaries. They must be clear, they must be firm, and they must be communicated as a natural part of life.

"Mommy, I hope Derrick[27] doesn't ever touch me again the way he did tonight."

Franny had just returned home from a conference in St. Louis. A Bahá'í friend had watched her daughter. Franny's heart was in her throat as she tried to silence a gasp of disbelief and a groan of anguish. Calming herself, she asked, "Where did Derrick touch you, Belinda?"

"Right here," she said, pointing to her pubic area.

"How do you feel about that?" Franny asked.

"I feel kind of yuckie," Belinda sighed.

"Do you want to talk about it? I have plenty of time right now."

Franny was encouraging her to open up and communicate any confusion, anger, or fear she might have because of her encounter with Derrick.

"No, I just want to go to bed and sleep right now."

"Well, when you feel like you're ready to talk about it, just tell me. I have a special friend who would enjoy talking to you about it. She knows how to make little girls feel special. And before you go to sleep, I want you to know that that yuckie feeling isn't about something you did, but was about something Derrick did to you. And I'm going to protect you so he will never touch you in that way again. Let's say some prayers and then you can go to sleep." Franny and Belinda said, "O God, guide me, protect me. Illumine the lamp of my heart and make me a brilliant star. Thou art the mighty and powerful."

She tucked Belinda in, smiled at her, then went to her room and screamed into her pillow. Her husband wasn't home. She had no one to process this event with. She cried while praying that her daughter would not be traumatized by this act of molestation. Sleep did not come easily.

The next morning she went into action. She called Derrick on the telephone. She was thankful that she had just recently learned how to use an "I-Statement."

"Hello, Derrick. I want you to know that I feel very angry that you touched my daughter in an inappropriate way and I want to know what your plans are so that you will never touch another child in this way and so that you will stop losing friends. I know that you were to come to my house for a meeting this weekend, but you are no longer welcome in my home. You are never to see my daughter again because I think that would be detrimental to her healing."

Derrick was silent on the other end of the phone and when Franny finished, he wept and said, "I'm so sorry. I will get some counseling."

Franny then reported the incident to the Local Spiritual Assembly. She did not tell anyone else. She did not tell Derrick's wife.

When Franny related this story to me, I learned that there were other children at the home of the man who molested her daughter. I advised Franny to inform Derrick's wife in order to make sure their children were protected. Derrick should not be trusted to volunteer that information to his wife. Franny said she would make sure this was done either by herself or the Local Spiritual Assembly.

Most important in this story is the fact that there existed a previously established environment of open communication and a trusting relationship between mother and daughter. This allowed Belinda to express—within 24 hours and *before it was buried*—whatever confusion or shame she experienced because of the encounter. It came out right away and it was worked out right away. Today Belinda is healthy and free of shame.

This story underscores the importance of teaching all children protective behaviors as they live in this degenerating society. Just because we are Bahá'ís does not mean we will escape the ills of our society.

If a child has been molested or abused, the legal authorities and Child Protection Services should be notified to enforce protection and sanctions. The child should be taught that the shame they feel as a result of the abuse was not about them but because of something that happened to them. They should be reassured that they are not bad; that they will be protected; and that they never have to see the person alone again.

If the child does not seem to be capable of sorting through his or her feelings, thoughts, and physical responses, then time and resources for that should be recommended, such as counseling with a therapist or social worker.

All children should be taught the difference between good touch, hurting touch, and *secret touch,* so that they can alert their parents or other adults when a hurting touch or a secret touch occurs. Note that I did not say "good touch/bad touch." Therapists and social workers have found that if they call sexual abuse or molestation "bad" touch, the children then think they are bad because they have participated in something "bad." The reasoning: if I feel bad, it must be true that I am.

Parents should name at least five people their child can go to if someone is doing secret touch: Mom, Dad, teacher, friend, aunt, etc. They should also be told that if one person doesn't believe them, they are to keep on telling someone else until someone listens. Children should also be taught that, "there is nothing so terrible that we can't say it out loud to someone."

We teach children the dangers of going into the streets, touching hot things, hurting others' feelings, and so on. We must also alert children to this type of danger without alarming them.

Domestic Violence in the Bahá'í Community

Behind closed doors and beyond whispers, domestic abuse exists. It shows no discrimination along lines of age, sex, race, religion, or social status. It includes everything from verbal bashing to sexual abuse to physical assault. Left untended, it will escalate to possibly fatal results. As with all forms of violence, it affects not only the physical body, but also the spirit, mind, and emotional state. It leads to the destruction of the family, the "basic unit of society."[28]

The Bahá'í teachings are very clear when they state that marriage is a "fortress for well-being."[29] The Universal House of Justice emphatically states, in a letter written on its behalf to a National Spiritual Assembly, that domestic violence is contrary to the Bahá'í teachings on marriage, and that, in effect, it destroys this "fortress."

> ... the stress laid in the statements of Bahá'u'lláh and 'Abdu'l-Bahá on love and harmony as the hallmark of marriage, and in view of 'Abdu'l-Bahá's exhortation that each member of the family must uphold the rights of others, makes it clear that violence in the family is contrary to the spirit of the Faith and a practice to be condemned. It is clear that no husband should subject his wife to abuse of any kind, whether emotional, mental or physical. Such a reprehensible action would be the very antithesis of the relationship of mutual respect and equality enjoined in the Bahá'í writings—a relationship governed by the principles of consultation and devoid of the use of any form of abuse, including force, to compel obedience to one's will.[30]

Abuse: Some Accounts and What to Do

Grace, badly beaten, her eye swollen shut, and her mouth bleeding, lay down on the bed to rest after she called the police. In a state of fury her former husband went methodically from one window to the next, smashing the glass as he angrily circled the house. Helpless, she wept as she waited for the police to arrive. They were there in two minutes, and he was arrested. She called Ginny, the secretary of her Local Spiritual Assembly, and asked for an appointment with the Assembly.

We could weep at such a vivid description of abuse that is such a far cry from the principle of the equality of men and women, as well as contrary to the fundamental Bahá'í principle that conflicts should be resolved through consultation, not violence. And we raise the question, how is it possible for one human being to treat another in this way?

> Often the perpetrator of domestic violence views himself (or herself) as a person who has a problem which he or she has tried to solve in other ways which have failed, therefore, violence is now being used as a last resort. . . .
> This violence against another human being may also be the result of the aggressor thinking they have superior rights over another human being.[31]

It is unthinkable that a husband, or for that matter a wife, would batter a spouse, it is so contrary to the Bahá'í Teachings. Yet even this is addressed by our institutions of authority because of the cycle of violence that has engulfed those who respond compulsively to challenges in a relationship.

> The use of force by the physically strong against the weak, as a means of imposing one's will and fulfilling one's desires, is a flagrant transgression of the Bahá'í Teachings. There can be no justification for anyone compelling another, through the use of force or through the threat of violence, to do that to which the other person is not inclined. 'Abdu'l-Bahá has written, "O ye lovers of God! in this, the cycle of Almighty God, violence and force, constraint and oppression, are one and all condemned."
> Let those who, driven by their passions or by their inability to exercise discipline in the control of their anger, might be tempted to inflict violence on another human being, be mindful of the condemnation of such disgraceful behavior by the Revelation of Bahá'u'lláh.
> . . . No Bahá'í husband should ever beat his wife, or subject her to any form of cruel treatment; to do so would be an unacceptable abuse of the marriage relationship and contrary to the Teachings of Bahá'u'lláh.[32]

When a Bahá'í wife finds herself in such a situation [of domestic violence] and feels it cannot be resolved through consultation with her husband, she could well turn to the Local Spiritual Assembly for advice and guidance . . .[33]

Often with cases of domestic violence, individuals do not take their problems to the Assembly for a number of reasons. They may be embarrassed to do so as it will indicate that they have been violated as a human being; they feel it might bring shame to their families; they are frightened if they do, domestic violence will be even more severe; or they may feel that the Assembly is not competent in dealing with this problem of theirs. There may be other reasons. If individuals feel that they cannot tell their Local Assembly, they should go to the National Spiritual Assembly. Such a situation may arise if, for example, one of the parties to the conflict is serving on the Local Spiritual Assembly. The universal House of Justice also notes that a person in this situation "might . . . find it highly advantageous to seek the assistance of competent professional counsellors."[34]

Some communities may advise the couple to separate and to seek treatment from professional counseling services. It is suggested that Local Spiritual Assemblies also follow this method of treating domestic violence. The Universal House of Justice has said:

There is no obligation on a wife, who is being subjected to beating by her husband, to continue living with him; she has the freedom to leave him and live in a separate domicile if she feels it necessary to do so.[35]

If, alternatively, the couple is counseled to remain together to try and reconcile their differences, there can be no guarantee that the violence will not recur, in which case the Assembly could appear, inadvertently, to be condoning it. If the couple separate, however, the role of the Assembly can then become that of providing an independent forum within which the couple can come together and try to resolve their differences. It is imperative that action be taken and the couple undergoes counseling. If no intervention takes place the 'cycle of violence' may very well repeat itself. This may be obscured by remorse and guilt; or a feeling of helplessness and self-blame on the victim's part, followed by apparent good relations between the couple which they confirm. However, left untreated, violence has the possibility of surfacing again.[36]

The Local Spiritual Assembly can help those who are currently being traumatized by domestic violence in many ways. Oscar Arrambide, a Bahá'í in Texas who counsels those who are battered, offers these suggested guidelines:

1. Listen, listen, listen!
The traumatized are hurting and in pain and need to be listened to. There are survivors and victims who feel nobody cares—show them you do.

2. Know the resources in your community.
Find out what agencies can help the victim and abuser. Know what counseling agencies are available. Find out the provisions of the laws on family violence in your state.

3. Do not band-aid consultation.
Take your time. Take consultation deeper than just offering suggestions and quotations. Let the victim talk it all out. Help the victim think through all options. You may need to consult with the other side, too.

4. Ask the victim what kind of help he or she needs.
Some victims are able to tell you what they need. Those victims who cannot tell you need special help.

5. Establish contact with experts.
Contract with licensed counselors. Get the training needed to deal with problems that you have no knowledge of how to handle.

6. Put yourself in their place.
Try to understand their feelings and situation.

7. Do not make judgments.
A victim feels worthless and does not need to feel worse. Empower the victim to take control of his or her life. Avoid the words, "You should do this . . .," and the like. Say: "I think it would be in your best interest to . . ." Or, "What do you think about this idea?"

8. Your decision needs to have power of enforcement.
A well-thought-out decision needs to be enforceable. A well-thought-out decision needs to be time-limited. A well-thought-out decision needs both victim and abuser to participate in carrying it out.

9. Be supportive of both the victim and the abuser.
Establish a men's support group. Establish a women's support group.[37]

Alyce Blue, a Bahá'í who is a domestic violence counselor and who has worked in shelters in Asia as well as in the southern United States and on Native American Reservations in Minnesota, also has a number of excellent suggestions for helping the victim. She says, "Always begin by assessing the amount, the kind of violence, and the extent of danger that the victim currently faces." In addition:

- Listen and believe the victim when the victim seeks help. Take any report of violence, sexual abuse, or molestation seriously.

- Be clear and specific about options when you feel the situation is lethal. Is the victim in jeopardy by seeing you? Does the victim have a network of support? Does the victim have a place to stay? Does the victim have a clear and safe plan for leaving the house when the victim senses danger?

- Do not demand instant decision making or contribute to unrealistic expectations. Let the victim know that you and others will help but that there are no quick, easy answers.

- Be prepared for ambivalent or fluctuating feelings as different aspects of the marital relationship, the violent incidents, or the abuser's behavior is recalled.

- Help the victim identify and label feelings. This may be difficult since a common coping mechanism for victims is numbness of feelings or helplessness which camouflages anger and other strong emotions.

- Do not deny any of the victim's feelings, such as anger at men/women/spouse, or feelings of love for the spouse.

- Help the victim identify how violence has changed or affected their behavior. Identify the behaviors and substances, such as tranquilizers, alcohol or other drugs which may be in use to help cover the pain.

- Help the victim identify strengths as well as weaknesses. Do not encourage a constant focus on the victim's role. Encourage the victim to identify some positive roles for his/her life, self and children, and some activities and methods of making the victim feel good. Religious beliefs may also be a source of strength.

- Assist the victim in identifying ways to solve problems. Problem solving begins with a response to or a recheck of the victim's safety. Once safety is ensured, develop a list of needs, establishing small steps for meeting each one. The victim must learn and perform every step of this process himself/herself. Helpers can clarify and support, but most must resist the urge to do too much because then the information and skills are not transferred to the victim.

- Help the victim identify their expectations in each situation and the marital relationship to strengthen confidence in their own perceptions and knowledge.

- Teach the victim how to obtain help, how to be an advocate for herself/himself when dealing with the systems such as: welfare, police, courts, schools, and medical agencies. (Volunteers or former battered persons can provide emotional support or can model how to get help.)

- Provide the victim with the support of other victims, especially those who were once battered. Without a connection with persons who share the battering experience, it is easy for the victim to remain somewhat isolated and to continue to feel guilt.

- Keep doors open. Let the victim know that whatever they do or decide about the relationship, it is their decision and that you will not judge them for returning to the relationship or for trying again to cope with it. Instead, express concern for them and their safety and the value you see in them.

- Be prepared to say the same things many times. Know that, although it may be frustrating, every time you take time to explain and work on the problem, you help to build up the victim's self-image a little bit more. The victim may be able to take further steps down the road because of your help.[38]

Conclusion

With this look at the broad range of circumstances that must be faced in a growing community, the Local Spiritual Assembly and caring individual should at least be able to speak confidently to those in need, without making unrecoverable errors. These instructions and tools will prove to be extremely valuable in supporting your efforts to bring the traumatized to those professionals who can best offer therapy, resources, and guidance.

Bear in mind that both the victim and the perpetrator of domestic violence have been disempowered. A study of "cognitive distortions"[39] which block accurate thinking is necessary to free some of their powers. Remember that the power of imagination can either help the traumatized or the perpetrator discover solutions to their problems or it could result in destructive fantasies that further block useful powers. The power of identity is dependent upon the development of the power of utterance. Consultation is rendered useless without the power of utterance. The power of reasoning grows exponentially with the freedom to use the power of utterance. It must be freed! The victim's power of perception may need to be validated endlessly if it has been discounted by the perpetrator in the continuous cycle of violence. Their power of intellectual investigation of truth will need to be encouraged if they are to take command in the process of seeking resources. The power of discernment must be stimulated by the writings on violence and force so that the perpetrator will come to know how gravely unacceptable is his or her behavior. And both the victim and the perpetrator will need to understand the difference between true intimacy and boundary enmeshment. Directing both parties to the specific writings of Bahá'-u'lláh that grant permission to develop and use their powers will be a great assistance for future growth and for emotional and mental stability, as well as for spiritual happiness.

Chapter 7

The Current Perpetrators of Abuse

Introduction

It is not easy to break through centuries of errors in judgment, attitudes that protect the perpetrator of abuse, acceptance of the status quo, uninformed opinions, and all-out denial about sexual abuse, domestic violence, and physical abuse. The institutions of the Bahá'í Faith have made great strides in addressing these issues forthrightly and have greatly expanded consciousness within the Bahá'í community. This chapter will seek to clarify the nuances of our responsibility to protect the victim of abuse and the consequences for the offender.

That which has remained a secret must be brought into the light, not only for the sake of the innocent victim, but for the sake of the transgressor. Both need to be treated, and both need to be healed. Society must become a conscious guardian of the present and future generations of those who are dependent and defenseless.

The Perpetrators of Abuse

In the Bahá'í Faith, abuse is named a "reprehensible action," the "very antithesis of the relationship of mutual respect and equality enjoined in the Bahá'í writings."* So what are the consequences and actions for those who perpetrate abuse?

It is not up to us as individual members of the Bahá'í community to determine punishment of other community members for actions that are contrary to the teachings of the Bahá'í

---

*From a letter written on behalf of the Universal House of Justice to the National Spiritual Assembly of Australia, dated April 12, 1990, in *Local Spiritual Assembly Handbook*, p. 261.

Faith. Justice is meted out by our institutions. But what do we do if we know of a perpetrator of abuse? As Bahá'ís we are enjoined by our Central Figures to overlook the faults of others. But electing a sin-covering eye does not mean the perpetrator of sexual abuse should escape justice. Exposing a perpetrator of sexual abuse protects children from violence and molestation. Sexual abuse is a crime! Those who abuse others will suffer both spiritual and legal consequences. They cannot avoid the consequences of a shameful exposure, the possibility of watching their marriage dissolve, of losing parental rights, or of serving time in jail. This is a powerful motivation to change. People make rational decisions to change because of the hope of greater self-fulfillment and the desire to avoid pain and discomfort.[1]

But exposure is not enough. The Local Spiritual Assembly must become aware of their authority to effect change in the abuser. Oscar Arrambide, a domestic violence counselor in Texas, says he counsels men who are arrogant about their own actions as perpetrators of abuse:

> . . . even that does not describe them. They will manipulate people to believe what they [the abusers] want them to believe. The Bahá'í victims who have contacted me through a newspaper ad told me that their husbands manipulated the Local Spiritual Assemblies to side with [the abusers]. This has caused a sense of hopelessness in some of the victims.[2]

Local Spiritual Assemblies in *every state of the United States* must contact their State Departments of Children and Family Services (or a similar organization) to learn the legal parameters that govern the reporting of even suspected cases of incest, sexual abuse, or molestation. Every doctor, therapist, counselor, teacher, and hospital is by law required to report such information. As a legal governing entity, the Local Spiritual Assembly is also subject to this requirement.

In *Developing Distinctive Bahá'í Communities* it is stated:

> If an Assembly is handling a case in which the state has exclusive interest (such as child abuse, sexual molestation,

battering, severe neglect, etc.), it must be careful not to interfere with the established legal procedures. For example, most states require all suspected cases of child abuse to be reported to the civil authorities. In those states, Bahá'í institutions would be legally required to report all such cases to the appropriate social service agencies. In addition, many states require persons in certain positions, i.e. teachers, doctors, etc., to report these types of cases.[3]

The Local Spiritual Assembly cannot dismiss such reports without following through. As they are not qualified to conduct a thorough investigation, and because they are not trained in this field, they can be easily manipulated. Better to place it in the hands of the experts.

Further, the *Local Spiritual Assembly Handbook,* published in Australia, advises:

> It is vital that the Assembly not be influenced by the personalities or the public perception of the individuals and their standing in the community and that they be objective in their assessment of the problem.
>
> The Local Spiritual Assembly needs to be optimistic about the resolution of the problem due to the all-encompassing Bahá'í belief in the potential within each individual for the transformation of human character. Many of the issues raised can be traced back to lack of spirituality in the lives of believers and recognition of this enables the Assembly to be enthusiastic about positive strategies for change.
>
> Trust by the couple in the Assembly. This results in effective change. To achieve this state the Assembly needs to ensure absolute confidentiality and to be impartial in its dealings with both parties. While it is a function of the Assembly to administer justice it is also a function to be a loving shepherd to all parties and not to rush to judgment without full knowledge of the facts.[4]

The Law of Justice

All Bahá'ís are encouraged to develop a virtuous attitude as part of their ongoing spiritual transformation. But some of us make errors in how we perceive the way the virtue of forgiveness, for example, relates to the question of physical abuse, sexual abuse, and domestic violence. Although we are at the ready to forgive those who are psychologically "sick," we must exercise caution in this area. The abuse of others is a spiritual sickness that needs to be confronted and named as a crime so that measures can be taken to protect the defenseless. In this quotation, 'Abdu'l-Bahá verifies that a "crime" requires consequences:

> If a person commit a crime against you, you have not the right to forgive him . . . [5]

And in *The Advent of Divine Justice* we find:

> The canopy of existence . . . resteth upon the pole of justice, and not of forgiveness, and the life of mankind dependeth on justice and not on forgiveness.[6]

And again in *Bahá'í World Faith*:

> It is not advisable to show kindness to a . . . tyrant, a traitor or a thief, because kindness encourages him to become worse and does not awaken him.[7]

Oscar Arrambide clarifies further the principles of forgiveness and justice:

> In other writings by 'Abdu'l-Bahá and Shoghi Effendi, it is made clear that individuals are to forgive, as individuals, but that they must seek justice as members of the social order. You may find it in your heart—in fact, you *must* find it— personally to forgive someone who has harmed you, rather than seek revenge, but you also have a duty to see that he or she is safely put away in jail (if need be) for the protection of society. This clarifies the apparent flaw that many find in the Christian teaching of "turning the other cheek." A confused Christian may ask what, then, is to stop the bully from bullying? The Bahá'í answer is the Law of Justice.[8]

Forgiveness does not mean reconciliation. There can be no reconciliation with a person who is denying the immoral acts they are perpetrating and refuses therapy to help end their sexual abuse of children, which, according to the Universal House of Justice, is a "perversion of human conduct."[9] Bahá'u'lláh forgave Mírzá Yaḥya. He did not reconcile with him, but He left the door open in the event that Mírzá Yaḥya might repent. True repentance includes humbling yourself, changing your behavior, and becoming responsible for your present and future moral choices.

The Prohibition Against Backbiting

Gossip and backbiting are painful to hear. Most of us feel alarmed in its presence and shrink away from participating in it. However, our minds and hearts can be torn with confusion about this teaching, and we can be consumed with doubts should the precious well-being of a child be hanging in the balance. When do we speak? To whom do we speak? When do we remain silent, especially when it is known that silence has for centuries protected the perpetrator and allowed the victim to suffer?

When misconstrued, this teaching may actually keep a victim from seeking aid.

> . . . regard backbiting as grievous error, and keep himself aloof from it's dominion, inasmuch as backbiting quencheth the light of the heart, and extinguisheth the life of the soul.[10]

Such statements might be wrongly taken as admonitions to suffer silently under injustice. However, the many references on justice are not ambiguous. On the contrary, they confirm with certitude how to proceed. In *Bahá'í Studies Notebook: The Divine Institution of Marriage,* it affirms,

> There is no Bahá'í writing that forbids giving testimony against a wrongdoer. As a matter of fact, the Law of Justice . . . demands it in order that peace and harmony may prevail in the community and human life and human rights be respected. On no account can the law against backbiting

be used to allow an abuser to escape justice or prosecution. This may be made very clear to the victim and references on justice used to give moral support.

The [Local Spiritual] Assembly can also assist the offender by invoking the law against backbiting to suppress gossip and keep a problem from becoming a community scandal. This makes it possible for the offender to seek help and make a new start without being condemned by the weight of a bad reputation.[11]

The Kitáb-i-Aqdas

Bahá'u'lláh offers lucid directions on how the Local Spiritual Assembly is to deal with those who commit crimes against children. In response to those who commit sexual acts outside of marriage, *which includes sexual abuse of defenseless children,* Bahá'u'lláh states in paragraph no. 49 of *The Kitáb-i-Aqdas*: "God hath imposed a fine on every adulterer and adulteress, to be paid to the House of Justice." In note 77 of *The Kitáb-i-Aqdas*, this statement is discussed as follows:

> In one of His Tablets, 'Abdu'l-Bahá refers to some of the spiritual and social implications of the violation of the laws of morality and, concerning the penalty here described, He indicates that the aim of this law is to make clear to all that such an action is shameful in the eyes of God and that, in the event that the offense can be established and the fine imposed, the principle purpose is the exposure of the offenders—that they are shamed and disgraced in the eyes of society. He affirms that such exposure is in itself the greatest punishment.[12]

Individuals should be aware that public exposure of the offender who is sexually abusing children or adolescents should always come from the governing Bahá'í institution. The individual has the responsibility to bring it to the attention of the Local Spiritual Assembly. The Local Spiritual Assembly then has the responsibility to bring it to the knowledge of the community if they deem it necessary and vital. This is a very important knowledge in that its purpose is to protect the innocent from one who is perpetrating a crime against children. The silence of authority has always protected the offender instead of the child. It takes wisdom and courage to deal with the conflict that may naturally result when the perpetrator is feeling shamed, angry, and trapped. It then becomes the responsibility of the community to refrain from gossip, but to be ever watchful in guarding the rights of the weak and defenseless, and to be willing to face conflict for them if necessary! Even if our first instinct in a conflict is to be passive or to flee, it is important to recognize that neither behavior will help children who need to be protected. As Bahá'ís, knowing the importance placed on interpersonal harmony, we may be inclined to avoid confrontation and conflict. We may not even always be aware of the need to set clear boundaries with others. Certainly, the Author of our Faith categorically forbids conflict and contention.[13] And although a Local Spiritual Assembly or an individual cannot hide from the conflict that will result from seeking justice for children, we are told to do so in as loving a way as possible, and to do it through the institutions.

To further illumine our understanding, Bahá'u'lláh reveals to us the sadness in His soul in the following quotation:

> We shrink, for very shame, from treating of the subject of boys. Fear ye the Merciful, O peoples of the world! Commit not that which is forbidden you in Our Holy Tablet, and be not of those who rove distractedly in the wilderness of their desires.[14]

In note no. 134 at the end of *The Kitáb-i-Aqdas*, a word of explanation is offered regarding this quotation: "The word translated here as 'boys' has, in this context, in the Arabic original, the implication of pederasty."[15] Although boys are specifically referred to, this statement may be taken as Bahá'u'lláh's prohibition of the sexual abuse of children in general. In a letter from the Universal House of Justice, the following is offered:

> It is difficult to imagine a more reprehensible perversion of human conduct than the sexual abuse of children, which

finds its most debased form in incest. At a time in the fortunes of humanity when, in the words of the Guardian, *"The perversion of human nature, the degradation of human conduct, the corruption and dissolution of human institutions, reveal themselves . . . in their worst and most revolting aspects,"* and when *"the voice of human conscience is stilled,"* when *"the sense of decency and shame is obscured,"* the Bahá'í institutions must be uncompromising and vigilant in their commitment to the protection of the children entrusted to their care, and must not allow either threats or appeals to expediency to divert them from their duty. A parent who is aware that the marriage partner is subjecting children to such sexual abuse should not remain silent, but must take all necessary measures, with the assistance of the Spiritual Assembly or civil authorities if necessary, to bring about an immediate cessation of such grossly immoral behavior, and to promote healing and therapy.[16]

In addition, an article containing guidance on dealing with situations of child abuse appeared in *The American Bahá'í* on April 9, 1994:

Assembly Must Report Child Abuse to Authorities

If a Spiritual Assembly suspects or becomes aware of a case of child abuse within the Bahá'í community, it should immediately report the matter to the appropriate civil authorities (such as Child Protective Services, the Department of Child and Family Services, depending on the state). Bahá'í institutions should generally not try to investigate cases of child abuse on their own, as they lack the resources, authority and expertise to do so.

Furthermore, although the consultation of a Local Spiritual Assembly is held to be legally privileged information (such as the consultation between a lawyer and client or between priest and penitent), the law in all 50 states now requires that any person or institution that becomes aware of a suspected ongoing case of child abuse must report the matter immediately.

Bahá'í institutions, as in the case of accusations of murder, fraud, burglary, rape, etc., must rely, in the first instance, upon the judgment of the police and legal system. If a Bahá'í should be convicted of child abuse, typically his or her administrative rights are removed as a result. If the individual applies for the restoration of administrative rights after release from incarceration, restrictions are usually placed on that person's contact with children, depending on the evaluation of psychiatrists or other qualified mental health personnel.

In the case of those who are not convicted or who are, for various reasons, not put on trial for child abuse, the National Spiritual Assembly may, on rare occasions, in the face of clear and sufficient evidence, remove an individual's administrative rights. Obviously, the evidence in such cases must be carefully weighed and documented, including whether or not there is a history of such behavior and whether there seems to be a likelihood that the individual may repeat the behavior in the future.

Because the Bahá'í institutions are not expert in such matters, the opinion of a competent mental health professional should be solicited, where possible. The Local Assembly investigating such a case must endeavor to consult with the alleged perpetrator, the victim, and any witnesses, and to obtain any documentation available from civil authorities or agencies that have looked into the matter.

While the National Assembly does believe that prayer and diligent effort to follow the teachings of Bahá'u'lláh can have a transforming effect on an individual's character, there may also be psychological and/or medical facets to an individual's behavior. In such cases, the Bahá'í institutions should recommend that the individual concerned seek the counsel and help of a physician or mental health professional.

There are no specific deepening courses on how Bahá'ís or Bahá'í institutions should cope with problems of child abuse, incest or related issues. However, we encourage Assemblies facing such problems to consult with the

National Spiritual Assembly about appropriate measures to take from a Bahá'í perspective, as well as to consult with trained medical and mental health professionals when confronted with such a problem.[17]

To sum up: The individual and the Local Spiritual Assembly are responsible for setting firm boundaries for those who use children for sexual gratification or abuse them in any manner. Now that the Kitáb-i-Aqdas has been distributed and there are numerous letters from our institutions of authority, we have firm guidance that confirm how these tragedies should be addressed.

Help for the Perpetrator of Abuse

Whether perpetrators have been raised in a rigid authoritarian system or a permissive system, they may need to deal with their rebelliousness in order to get well. They need to be directed back to rules, limits, and controls that are balanced with a responsible freedom.

They have been conditioned to be externally controlled. They must be taught that God's rules, limits, and controls are meant to be an internalized means of self-government and that God's laws are a mercy to us through which He provides justice and protection for the rights of all the peoples of the world.

The Local Spiritual Assembly and other institutions of authority are there to provide open discussion and firm guidance that directs the Bahá'í perpetrator of abuse to problem-solving assistance, as well as to provide safety and justice for victims and to guard the trusting, the unaware, and the unsuspecting. This firm guidance may look like the kind of punishment or external control they have always experienced, but the purpose of the exertion of such authority by Bahá'í institutions is to awaken the conscience of the Bahá'í perpetrator to make correct moral and behavioral choices based on the writings of Bahá'u'lláh. It is not authority seeking merely to prevail or to exercise absolute power.

And it can be the hope of Bahá'í institutions of authority that this awakening of conscience, coupled with the fear of God, will create the kind of awareness that will promote forethought of consequences resulting in the use of internal controls the Bahá'í perpetrator of physical or sexual abuse lacks. Perhaps it will even awaken the faculty of shame.

The many powers that are listed in the Bahá'í writings can also benefit the perpetrator of abuse, since part of their difficulty is that they have been developmentally disempowered by the abuse issues from their own childhood. They need to know what powers they lack, what powers are distorted, and what powers are used for defense instead of transformation. They need to know how to recognize and reduce stress; how to deal with anger and powerlessness; how to set inner boundaries for their power of imagination in order to avoid out-of-control fantasies; and how to set boundaries for their outer behavior in community with others. They also need to become conscious that their power of identity is based upon sexuality and what steps are necessary toward developing an identity based upon spirituality. And ultimately, their powers of volition, perception, and discernment need to be transformed.

It must be remembered that the above section applies to current perpetrators of sexual abuse. The treatment of *former* perpetrators who have received counseling and worked through whatever issues were necessary for their healing should be based on the behavior they exhibit today, the guidance of their mental health professional, and the restrictions that have been placed on them by the court system.

A Final Word

The final word belongs to Bahá'u'lláh. He has reassured us in the Kitáb-i-'Ahd (the Book of the Covenant) that even our most grievous sins are forgiven; and that if we fear God and adhere to what is right, peace is ours, and the loftiness which is latent within us will be revealed:

> The aim of this Wronged One in sustaining woes and tribulations, in revealing the Holy Verses and in demonstrating proofs hath been naught but to quench the flame of hate and enmity, that the horizon of the hearts of men may be

illumined with the light of concord and attain real peace and tranquility. From the dawning-place of the divine Tablet the day-star of this utterance shineth resplendent, and it behoveth everyone to fix his gaze upon it: We exhort you, O peoples of the world, to observe that which will elevate your station. Hold fast to the fear of God and firmly adhere to what is right. Verily I say, the tongue is for mentioning what is good, defile it not with unseemly talk. God hath forgiven what is past. Henceforward everyone should utter that which is meet and seemly, and should refrain from slander, abuse and whatever causeth sadness in men. Lofty is the station of man! Not long ago this exalted Word streamed forth from the treasury of Our Pen of Glory: Great and blessed is this Day—the Day in which all that lay latent in man hath been and will be made manifest. Lofty is the station of man, were he to hold fast to righteousness and truth and to remain firm and steadfast in the Cause.[18]

Appendix I

Obedience

(An address given by Mr. Ian Semple on 26 July 1991 in the Reception Concourse of the Seat of the Universal House of Justice in connection with the Spiritual Enrichment Program at the Bahá'í World Center.)

The International Teaching Center has produced a wonderful compilation, which you've all received, of texts on the subject of obedience. I'm assuming that you're familiar with those, and therefore I want to approach the subject from a more general point of view—principally about obedience in relation to freedom of thought and also to discussing the importance of obedience both to the individual's spiritual development and to society as a whole.

Mankind has suffered appallingly from tyranny, throughout virtually its whole history, and obedience has often come to be equated with servility and acquiescence in oppression—or even worse, to be used as an excuse for taking part in oppression. You know, because of having lived in Israel for some time, how often this comes up when the question of the Holocaust is being discussed. Those who took part in the Holocaust said, "Well, I was just obeying orders; I am not the one to blame." Now, because of this history of oppression, obedience has become widely despised, and freedom and "rugged individualism" are prized as true goals of social life. What, then, are we to make of this statement of Bahá'u'lláh:

What mankind needeth in this day is obedience unto them
that are in authority, and a faithful adherence to the cord of
wisdom.[1]

To understand this we need to see the other side of the picture.
We need to appreciate the enormity of the problems mankind is
grappling with, which are caused by violent nationalism and
tribalism, by individual greed and ruthless competition in economic life, by unbridled permissiveness in morality, and by the
ever-growing incidence of crime and terrorism. These are all
distortions of freedom.

History has shown a tendency of mankind to oscillate between
extremes of tyranny and unbridled license, with a few happy periods in between when society has attained a moderate condition.
Now I think we need to recognize that in the Bahá'í teachings we
are not merely trying to attain a moderate balance between
freedom and obedience, but rather, through the teachings,
Bahá'u'lláh has shown us how we can freely give obedience to
the standard of truth so that obedience and freedom combine in
a harmonious whole. They no longer become antitheses of one
another.

To explore this concept I want to consider it in the light of five
processes:

1. The first is to accept oneself as the ultimate source of
   authority.
2. The second is to recognize one's own insufficiency.
3. The third is to validate a source of authority outside
   oneself.
4. The fourth is the process of understanding the requirements of that source of authority.
5. The fifth is the role of judgment in carrying out these
   requirements. The foundation for all development is to
   know oneself and to accept one's own responsibility for
   one's own life.

The next step is to learn that for a person to follow his own
inclinations in everything leads to chaos in his own life and in
society as a whole.

This leads one to search for an external source of authority, for what is truth. When one thinks one has found such a source it is essential to validate it. To fail to do so is to sacrifice one of the most fundamental rights and duties of a human being.

Having decided that a source of authority is valid, and that one wishes to obey it, one can only put this into practice if one understands what that source of authority requires.

Finally, unless one uses one's intelligence and good judgment in exercising one's obedience to authority, one may well end up doing the opposite of what it really intends.

All five of these processes require the exercise of one's reasoning powers. They are the negation of the concept of "blind obedience," and I believe that this concept of blind obedience is contrary to the spirit of the Faith. Obedience, for a Bahá'í is the free exercise of one's will to follow what one believes to be right. Blind obedience is the abdication of one's free will.

Recognition of the Individual's Responsibility

The responsibility placed by God on each individual soul to take command of his own life is stressed again and again in the Writings. Consider the following words of Bahá'u'lláh. The first passage is so familiar that we may be in danger of failing to ponder the many elements it contains, and that is why I am going to read it in a rather disjointed way:

> O SON OF SPIRIT!
> The best beloved of all things in My sight is Justice; turn not away therefrom if thou desirest Me, and neglect it not that I may confide in thee. By its aid thou shalt see with thine own eyes and not through the eyes of others, and shalt know of thine own knowledge and not through the knowledge of thy neighbor. Ponder this in thy heart; how it behooveth thee to be. Verily justice is My gift to thee and the sign of My loving-kindness. Set it then before thine eyes.[2]

Then we have these three other passages which develop the same theme:

Judge ye fairly the Cause of God, your Creator, and behold that which hath been sent down from the Throne on high, and meditate thereon with innocent and sanctified hearts. Then will the truth of this Cause appear unto you as manifest as the sun in its noon-tide glory. Then will ye be of them that have believed in Him.[3]

Lay not aside the fear of God, O ye the learned of the world, and judge fairly the Cause of this unlettered One to Whom all the Books of God, the Protector, the Self-Subsisting, have testified.[4]

He hath endowed every soul with the capacity to recognize the signs of God. How could He, otherwise, have fulfilled His testimony unto men, if ye be of them that ponder His Cause in their hearts. He will never deal unjustly with any one, neither will He task a soul beyond its power. He, verily, is the Compassionate, the All-Merciful.[5]

In these and a multitude of other passages, Bahá'u'lláh's first call to us is not to obey, but to use our minds, to judge fairly, to recognize, and then to believe and then to obey. He assures us that we have the capacity to recognize the truth and to follow it.

That ultimate authority resides in ourselves is true for any human being, whether he understands it or not. One may choose not to use this authority, to allow oneself to drift along like a bit of flotsam at the pull of the tide, or one may take charge of one's own life.

All too often nowadays we seek the cause for our actions in conditions and events which are beyond our control and which lie in our heredity, our upbringing or our circumstances. There is a certain truth in this, and I'm not saying these don't influence us, but in most cases it is a thoroughly debilitating excuse for doing the wrong thing and for failing to do what one fundamentally knows to be right.

One always has a choice of whether to bow to external events or to take steps to deal with them, whether to obey or disobey an external authority. To take steps to change our conditions may take effort, and we may decide not to make the effort—but that is our decision. Sometimes the alternative of disobeying an external authority brings with it such unpleasant consequences that one decides to obey in spite of one's disagreement. Even that is one's own decision. Ultimately, if one believes that the choice is serious enough, one will accept death rather than choose wrongly. But there's still always a choice, and I think this is very important because sometimes you find someone giving the excuse, "I'm sorry but I couldn't do the right thing—I'd have been shot!" That was a choice; you could have been shot.

In Iran it has been a perpetual astonishment to the persecutors of the Cause that Bahá'ís have made this choice, that rather than deny the Faith or breathe a word in denial of the faith they have accepted to be killed. Now this is where we have to be independent and strong.

So the first point of reference for any human being is himself, and his own God-given ability to decide. For an atheist or agnostic there is no central point of reference apart from himself and his own wishes and ideas. If he does not think at all, he will tend to be driven entirely by his likes and desires—in other words, not what he thinks is right, but just what he feels. Few people, however, live entirely at that subanimal level, fortunately. Sooner or later they begin to think about what is best for them. They begin to exercise their powers of choice. But usually they do not go far enough in the process. Many people merely exist from day to day, following the fashions and whims of the society in which they live, absorbing its prejudices and pursuing its standards.

For an individual to unthinkingly follow the promptings of his own self-centered desires necessarily brings him into conflict with others and increases the sum of misery in the world. Inevitably, if Number One comes first, and everybody is Number One, everybody is in conflict. Now, this is so whether or not he gets to the point of trying to dominate others for his own satisfaction. On the other hand, when people unthinkingly adhere to the prejudices of their society or of its leaders, this breeds animosity towards other groups. Both lead to spiritual decay and chaos. In the Seven Proofs, the Báb writes:

> In every nation thou beholdest unnumbered spiritual
> leaders who are bereft of true discernment, and among
> every people thou dost encounter myriads of adherents who
> are devoid of the same characteristic. Ponder for a while in
> thy heart, have pity on thyself and turn not aside thine
> attention from proofs and evidences.[6]

And, earlier in the same Book:

> Nay, by God, be thou neither a divine without discernment
> nor a follower without discernment, for both of these shall
> perish on the Day of Resurrection.[7]

Recognizing One's Own Insufficiency

As soon as a soul begins to wonder, not what he can do to please
himself, but what he ought to do; when he allows himself to
consider the difference between right and wrong; when he
begins to ponder the purpose of his life; when, in other words,
he becomes a person of discernment, he has taken the first step
away from true godlessness. Truth and Right and Justice and
Mercy are Names of God, and whoever seeks those is on the
path to seeking God. Many a self-styled atheist is not really an
atheist at all; he is merely a person who has seen beyond the
superficialities of traditional religion in his search for truth. I
think this is what we're seeing happen now in the East. People
who are theoretical atheists, many of them, have been at heart
truly spiritual people and merely haven't known what they were
looking for, and now they're finding it.

When he starts to think in that way, any person, atheist or not,
will begin to look around for examples, for patterns of behavior
that are apparently successful and which he can follow to
achieve similar success. He will start out with a whole range of
behavior patterns that he has learned from childhood. These he
may maintain, or he may discard them for other patterns. But
even then, unless he finds a central point of reference outside
himself, he will find it very difficult to rise above his current
level. It's like pulling yourself up by your own bootstraps—you
just can't do it.

So long as he remains the Center of his own universe, he

remains limited by his own nature. Alas, we have all met members of the Bahá'í community who have suffered from this limitation. Take, for example, someone who is afire for social justice and who, from his own experience in life and from ideas that he has drawn from others, has evolved a philosophy of social reform that is very close to the teachings of Bahá'u'lláh. When he meets the Faith, he finds a whole community of people with similar ideas. He declares himself a Bahá'í and is registered as a member of the community. If his attraction does not develop into true understanding of the teachings and into obedience to Bahá'u'lláh, he sooner or later meets with Bahá'í teachings which do not fit into his own philosophy, so he challenges them and tries to change the Faith to be closer to his own ideals. He does not succeed, so, in disillusionment, he leaves the Faith and drifts off to link up with others of like mind with whom, in due course, he comes again to disagree. Because he is self-centered he remains alone, in a sense, throughout his life. He may connect with some people but then break up again.

Thus, for the full development of the individual soul, and to enable it to work in harmony with other souls for the evolution of human society, it is essential for each human being to recognize the insufficiency of his own self and to seek a collective Center outside himself.

Validating an External Source of Authority

Unless one has a truly authoritative collective Center in harmony with the nature of the universe, no combination of individuals will endure. This is why mere social movements, and political parties, no matter how much loyalty they may inspire, are doomed to change, disintegration and ultimate collapse. But if one is to submit one's individual authority and freedom to an external authority, one has a duty to validate the source of that authority, whether it be the civil government, a political party or whatever.

The essential difference between religion and philosophy is that religion claims to be linked to God Himself, the Creator, Upholder and Mover of the universe. It is not merely a formulation of well-argued ideas, but a revelation of eternal truth. The authority it claims is absolute. This is both its strength and its danger. Its strength is that, when one is really linked to God, one is in harmony with all Truth and Justice and Beauty. Its danger is that, if one gives to a false prophet the obedience due to God Himself, one can descend into a perversion far worse than any that a philosophy can create. Consider the havoc wreaked by such charismatic leaders as Hitler. They have laid claim to absolute loyalty and obedience from their followers. Such leaders really create pseudo-religions rather than political parties. But even so, it is in the area of religion that validation of the source of authority has supreme importance.

No knowledge is more important to the individual soul than the understanding that, while one is responsible for seeking the truth and for distinguishing it from error, one also has an absolute obligation to follow the truth wherever it may lead. One must recognize that God cannot be bargained with.

Bahá'u'lláh encapsulates this truth in a sentence in one of His prayers:

> What power can the shadowy creature claim to possess when face to face with Him Who is the Uncreated?[8]

Now this is a very important, very difficult, and very uncomfortable truth. And here perhaps I can say something about the fear of God, because if one really thinks about God, it is a fearful prospect. You know, if one is an atheist, not having a God at all, one can blind oneself to some degree to the horror of the universe, by jogging along from day to day. But if one really thinks about it, the universe is an appalling place. Just look at the magnitude of the stars, just the sun itself with its sunspots, and think of oneself as this tiny little microbe crawling about on the surface of the earth. One is utterly powerless; what can one do? What can one do for the future? This is one of the theoretical problems that the Communists are facing. They had this marvelous idea that a person should be selfless, that an individual didn't live in a future life, there was no eternal life, but your future was in a future society. You served here to the best of your ability, you loved your fellow man, and you would create a world that would be a pattern of perfection on earth. That was your eternal life. The problem they found was that people began to realize this world doesn't last forever, either. Some time is going to come when this world will be destroyed. There is no permanent future in the perfection of this world. And when there's no future at all, one begins to wonder, "Well, why bother? Why do I sacrifice this seventy-odd years I have for something that's not going to last anyway?" Pascal, centuries ago, saw this problem: that the poverty and misery of a world without God is such that people cannot face it. They begin to seek distractions so they don't have to think about it. This is why a society, if it's an increasingly irreligious society, becomes more and more absorbed with amusement and diversion and thrills, because people cannot face the truth. Now then, to come to recognize that this world is not just a mass of atoms and molecules, but that there is something controlling it—there is God, in other words—can be for a time a nice philosophical concept, until you begin to treat it seriously. Then you realize that, if God is God, you can't say anything to God; you can't bargain with God. C. S. Lewis commented on this once. When he was drawn to recognize the reality of God he realized a demand was being made of him. God wasn't saying "Give me all or nothing." There was no choice; He said, "All." That's it, there is no alternative. God is God.

Now this is difficult but very important to realize. The tremendous bounty we get through the teachings of the Manifestations is to realize that this incomprehensible force behind the universe is not just a blind force but is the power of love, that the individual human soul has an importance in His sight and is within His care. This is a revolutionary idea and is, I think, at the heart of all religion.

But still one has to accept the fact that you can't bargain with God, and I recommend to any of you who have problems with the idea of accepting the concept of the fear of God, or are troubled by what seems to be injustice in the world, to study the Book of Job. It's a very old book, but it's all about this problem. Job is a very upright man, a very wealthy man, a very prosperous man, and in the story—of course the whole thing is an allegory—the Devil comes to God and says, "Look, he's only being so good because you're treating him so well. Take away all

his wealth and all his happiness, he won't obey you any more."
So God says, "All right," and He allows the Devil to take everything away from Job. And everything goes wrong. There comes a
whole series of friends and comforters, who are like the chorus
of the story, continually explaining to Job why things are going
wrong. They try to point out to him it's because he must have
sinned. "No, I haven't sinned. I'm not going to say I've sinned, I
haven't sinned! I'm not being punished for something I've
done." But he maintains all the way through his obedience to
God and his love for God. He says, "Even if He slays me I will
believe in Him." This whole pattern continues and we get these
different excuses for what's happening. And eventually Job himself is persuaded to ask God. And God's voice comes out of the
whirlwind:

> Then the Lord answered Job out of the whirlwind, and said,
> Who is this that darkeneth counsel by words without
> knowledge? Gird up now thy loins like a man; for I will
> demand of thee, and answer thou me. Where wast thou
> when I laid the foundations of the earth? Declare if thou hast
> understanding. Who hath laid the measures thereof, if thou
> knowest? or who hath stretched the line upon it? Whereup-
> on are the foundations thereof fastened? or who laid the
> corner stone thereof; When the morning stars sang together,
> and all the sons of God shouted for joy?[9]

There is no way that we can understand the nature of God or His
purposes, and we have to accept that. Now this is, shall we say,
the fear, and yet the exaltation of finally accepting the nature of
God. I have never forgotten the extraordinary perception of this
truth that was shown by a young man that I used to work with.
He was an articled clerk in a firm in which I was an accountant.
One day he began to inquire about the Faith and I gave him, I
think, *Bahá'u'lláh and the New Era;* and then we went on different
jobs. Then one day we were on the same job again, and he said,
"You know, I no longer have a choice. When I began to read this
book I realized it was so important that I have no alternative but
to study it and decide whether it is true or not. And if I find it's

true, I have no alternative but to follow it." Now there aren't that many people who have such deep perception so soon after hearing of the Faith—he hadn't even decided it was true. But he studied, and he decided, and he accepted the Faith. He understood very well the truth of Bahá'u'lláh's words:

> They should in no wise allow their fancy to obscure their judgment, neither should they regard their own imaginings as the voice of the Eternal.[10]

To admit that God is God, to accept that one is but a small part of His creation, and to understand that the fruition of the exercise of one's own independent authority is to surrender it to the authority of God, can be a very humbling and painful experience. Once done, however, it brings an accession of joy and strength that can scarcely be imagined, because one ceases to be alone, one becomes a willing integral part of the whole motion of the universe. It is a revelation of the mystery of sacrifice and of the astonishing fact that God is Love.

One of the dangers is that the joy that such self-surrender brings can be experienced by someone who surrenders to a false prophet as well as by someone who surrenders to the true Manifestation of God. Self-surrender is, itself, a virtue and you can get the same exaltation even by surrendering to the wrong thing. This is the danger. The methods by which we seek truth and accept it we know, and I shall not elaborate them here. You all remember the four criteria described by 'Abdu'l-Baha by which we can ascertain the truth: the senses, reason, tradition and inspiration. Each of these four standards is fallible, but we try our best to combine them all, and it is the guidance of God which is the final, infallible guidance.

What happens, however, if we have, to the best of our ability, satisfied our senses, our reason, the traditions we know, and we think we've been inspired, and have satisfied ourselves that a source of authority is valid, and have given it our obedience but, alas, we are mistaken? How are we to find out our mistake?

This brings us to the fourth process which I mentioned at the outset.

Understanding the Requirements of Authority

In his letter to the United National Special Palestine commission Shoghi Effendi stated that the Faith "enjoins upon its followers the primary duty of an unfettered search after truth."

This injunction is, at one and the same time, the safeguard against following a false prophet, and fountainhead of the light of consultation and the guarantee of the successful implementation of Bahá'u'lláh's command given in the Words of Paradise:

> Schools must first train the children in the principles of religion, so that the Promise and the Threat recorded in the Books of God may prevent them from the things forbidden and adorn them with the mantle of the commandments; but this in such measure that it may not injure the children by resulting in ignorant fanaticism and bigotry.[11]

We return again here to the antithesis between blind obedience and willing, conscious obedience, which I mentioned at the beginning of this talk. You may ask: "But why should we continue our independent search for truth after we have found it by accepting Bahá'u'lláh? Doesn't this indicate that we have doubts about His Station?" But do you think that finding Bahá'u'lláh is the end? Surely it is only the beginning. When one accepts that Bahá'u'lláh is the Manifestation of God, that He and His actions and His words are a perfect mirror of the nature of God, of His Truth and of His intentions for this age, then begins the long task of learning exactly what He is telling us, of putting His commands into practice in our lives, and of permitting the light of His Revelation to illumine our hearts and our understanding. This cannot take place if we close the shutters of our minds.

A true principle of action remains true no matter to whom it applies. The continuing exercise of our search for truth enables the followers of a true Prophet to draw ever closer to Him, to absorb His teachings and to integrate them into their lives. The same principle when applied by the followers of a false prophet will enable them, sooner or later, to discover his falsity. This is why it is false prophets who, above all, require blind obedience from their followers. They fear the truth—and for very good reason. But how can He who is Truth itself ever suffer from the pursuit of truth by His followers?

Then there is the matter of deepening ourselves in the teachings. How can we do this if we do not think about them, relate them to one another, try them out and study them in the light of experience? The teachings of Bahá'u'lláh are to suffice mankind for at least a thousand years. Can we imagine then that, without a lot of profound thinking, we shall really understand what He is saying and what He intends us to do?

It is only through independent, clear thinking about the vast range of the teachings that one can foster the growth of one's understanding.

But the texts are not our only source of guidance. Bahá'u'lláh has also given us consultation as our guide. To make this work we must exercise freedom of thought, frankness of expression, courtesy and obedience. Without the exercise of unfettered search after truth, and without obedience to its conclusions, consultation would be abortive.

So we have established the need for the use of an unfettered search after truth in understanding the requirements of authority. What are we to do when we find ourselves unable to accept those requirements? This can happen at various levels, and is a problem that should be squarely faced and tackled:

1. There may be a law of Bahá'u'lláh Himself which we either fail to understand or feel averse to obeying.
2. There may be a principle of the Faith or an instruction of the Guardian or of the Universal House of Justice which causes us great inconvenience or even danger to obey.
3. There may be a decision of a Spiritual Assembly which we are convinced is wrong.

How are we to react in such cases? They all lead back, I believe to the earlier part of the process, the validation of the source of authority. If we have trouble with understanding or obeying a law of Bahá'u'lláh Himself, we should not balk from examining the basis of our faith. We have accepted Bahá'u'lláh as the

Manifestation of God for reasons which we were convinced were valid. What does this one disagreement with His Writings signify? Is it sufficiently serious to throw into doubt all the evidence on which I have accepted Him in the first place, or is it an indication of a shortcoming in myself? If one finds that one's faith in Bahá'u'lláh is not shaken, and that it is merely the particular law that is a problem, one should obey on the basis of faith. Now I want to stress: this is not blind faith or blind obedience. 'Abdu'l-Baha has said:

> By Faith is meant, first, conscious knowledge, and second, the practice of good deeds.[12]

We have a solidly based reliance on Bahá'u'lláh as a source of authority in all things. Sometimes we can go forward in clear understanding of what He wants us to do. Sometimes we are left in the dark because our understanding has not yet grown sufficiently. The light that enables us to go forward through such dark patches is our faith in Him, our conscious knowledge that, in spite of immediate appearances, He is right, and He really does know better than we do. This knowledge enables us to act with full confidence accordingly and I stress this "full confidence." It isn't reluctant obedience to a law that one disagrees with; it is full-hearted obedience to a law one cannot understand but knows must be right. As Shoghi Effendi wrote:

> Are we to doubt that the ways of God are not necessarily the ways of man? Is not faith but another word for implicit obedience, whole-hearted allegiance, uncompromising adherence to that which we believe is the revealed and express will of God, however perplexing it might at first appear, however at variance with the shadowy views, the impotent doctrines, the crude theories, the idle imaginings, the fashionable conceptions of a transient and troublous age? If we are to falter or hesitate, if our love for Him should fail to direct us and keep us within His path, if we desert Divine and emphatic principles, what hope can we any more cherish for healing the ills and sicknesses of this world?[13]

The authority of the Guardian and the Universal House of Justice go back to the authority of Bahá'u'lláh Himself, so similar principles apply. One should obey them because one knows that they are divinely guided. I can recall more than one occasion on which I found myself either unable to understand or in disagreement with a decision of the Universal House of Justice. You know, the House of Justice doesn't always have unanimous decisions; it has majority decisions sometimes. Such a situation is not surprising of course. The House of Justice is infallible, but individual human beings aren't, so it's only logical that sometimes one should initially disagree with a decision that is reached. In all cases, naturally, I have accepted the decision and after a lapse of time I have always found why the House of Justice was right and I was wrong. The interesting thing is that it isn't only that it was for reasons that I didn't recognize at the time—"All right, that was what I misunderstood in the consultation, I now know what was right"—but sometimes even because of things that I could not have known at the time the decision was made. The ways of God, again, are mysterious, even when they come through His institutions. One cannot always expect to know everything at the outset.

Such experiences cause one to grow spiritually and enrich one's understanding to a unique degree. Intelligent and open-eyed obedience, therefore, promotes the growth of the soul.

Obeying a Spiritual Assembly which one believes to be wrong can be much more difficult. Here one obeys because of the overriding principle of upholding unity in the Faith. At the same time, if one judges the matter to be serious enough, one can always appeal the decision. Here again one must use wisdom. One has the right to appeal a decision, but one should consider not only one's own interest or the principle of the matter, but also the interests of the Cause. Is it right to occupy the time of the Assembly by insistently pursuing the point, even if one is sure that its decision is wrong, or is it better to pass it over and allow the Assembly to carry on with its main task, which is the teaching of the Cause of God? Sometimes it's right, sometimes it's wrong; sometimes one should insist, sometimes one should let it go. Again, it's a matter of judgment and good reason. So, here you come to the question of the role of reason in carrying out the commands of a source of authority.

The Role of Judgment in Carrying Out Commands

There are two different sources of authority one needs to think of here, because they are a little bit different. One is an issuer of commands, and the other is laws and regulations.

The difference between these is that a specific command from a source of authority is often quite clear, explicit and related to a particular matter, while a law or regulation is usually a more general commandment and its application to a specific case may need study and correlation with other regulations.

An interesting instance of the difference between these kinds of authority arose during the 1960s in America. You know, that was a time when there was great tension between the races, and the Bahá'ís were very much involved in the whole question of challenging color prejudice and establishing unity as far as they could, both within the Bahá'í community and outside it. The problem that was put to the House of Justice by the believers was: What happens if you're in one of the southern states where there's a law that prohibits a certain degree of association between people of different colors, but it so happens that this has got to the point now where the non-Bahá'ís are debating this law? Do the Bahá'ís have to obey it because we obey the civil law and it's a principle to obey the government, no matter which one it is? The House of Justice said, no, the Bahá'ís should carry out the principles of the Faith as far as they can, but if a person in authority says, "Don't do it," you don't do it. In other words, if the law says that whites and blacks shouldn't be around together, the Faith obviously says they should be. All right, they should go around together. But if a policeman comes up and says, "You sit in different places," you go and sit in different places. There is a difference between the law as it is written and the law as it is enforced, and this comes into play in many relations between the Bahá'í Faith and civil law. This came up, I would imagine, in similar situations in Nazi Germany. I am told that there, for example, when the Nazi authorities instructed the Bahá'ís to segregate their meetings between Jews and non-Jews, their solution was simply to stop having meetings. You can get around such problems in various ways.

Then there is the matter of obeying laws and principles of the Faith when to do so causes one difficulty or even suffering. As I have said, it is often obedience through faith, and accepting unpleasant choices, which make us grow spiritually and morally, and in our understanding. Such obedience also has an effect on the community as a whole. It produces a society which is united, loving, firmly righteous and courageous, but entirely free from "ignorant fanaticism and bigotry." This is the difficult balance: to be firm, to be principled, but not to be fanatical, and not to be bigoted.

One of the truths that one must accept is that life is not easy. It was not meant to be easy. If we acknowledge and accept this and work with it, we grow and progress through all trials and tribulations. This is a very profound realization. I think it was Carl Jung who attributed a great deal of psychic illness to the attempt of people to avoid what he called "legitimate pain." You see, all growth in life causes pain at certain stages. Think of the pain of adolescence, when we don't know how to cope with suddenly becoming adult. And when you marry, two people coming to live together, there's pain involved. And Jung, I think, put his finger on a very important point: to try to avoid legitimate pain produces psychic breakdown, and this is so in society as a whole. But it can make one seem somewhat ruthless, at times, if one goes ahead with obedience and acceptance of pain.

True obedience, thus, is not servility. It requires courage and endurance; and an essential element of obedience is the exercise of judgment in carrying out the requirements of the authority one has accepted.

Whether the source of authority in a particular instance is an instruction from an authoritative body or the requirements of a law, it is seldom possible for it to cover all possibilities and eventualities.

I remember reading a story once of a man who was particularly fond of one of his suits—men very often like their old suits and try to hang onto them forever—but as it was quite worn he couldn't hang onto it any longer, so he went to a tailor and told him to make an exact copy. The tailor duly did so, and said he had tried to make as good a copy as he possibly could, but apologized that he had had some difficulty in exactly reproducing the coffee-stain on the front of the jacket! This is the sort of problem that the Works Office is facing all the time. In this case, when you're repairing a Holy Place, you do want to reproduce it exactly as it is. When you have two windows next to each other, one a little bit smaller than the other, you don't want some bright person to come along and say, "It could be a bit more beautiful if we had them both the same size." You want the new one smaller than the other, exactly as the old one was. On the other hand, if we are replacing a leaky drainpipe, we do not want the new pipe to leak like the old one did. This is where you have to exercise good judgment, and it's astonishing how often in life you'll find that in just such cases people do not use good judgment, and it drives you crazy when you give what you think have been very clear instructions and the person comes back with something absolutely haywire, and says, "But you told me to!" And you know you told him to, but you wish he'd used his good sense and done it differently.

These are extreme examples, but the same principle arises continually in carrying out the laws of the Faith. When to be strict, when to be lenient, which exceptions are justifiable and which are not. How to be forbearing without sacrificing principles, how to be righteous without being fanatical. Generally speaking, it is a good guideline to be very strict with oneself and lenient with others. In the Second Ṭaráz Bahá'u'lláh writes:

> This Wronged One exhorteth the peoples of the world to observe tolerance and righteousness, which are two lights amidst the darkness of the world and two educators for the edification of mankind. Happy are they who have attained thereto and woe betide the heedless.[14]

The paralleling of tolerance and righteousness makes this, I think, a very interesting passage.

Here again, one is forced back on the principle of the ultimate responsibility of the individual. We should accept that God has given us minds to use, He has given us free will, and He has exhorted us to exercise wisdom and good judgment. This is one of the pains in life that we must accept.

I characterize it as a pain because we must be careful not to misuse this freedom as a license to disobedience. In one of the letters written on behalf of the Guardian his secretary gives the sobering warning that "We must be hopeful of God's Mercy but not impose upon it."

But there are valid cases where wise judgment would say to a person: "In this case I would be justified in doing what would normally be unacceptable." Some believers, fearing to accept this responsibility, ask the Universal House of Justice to grant an exception. This, of course, it often cannot do, because to do so would have far wider implications than that one case. But I remember more than one occasion when the House of Justice had to answer such a question, and the comment has been made: "We do wish he'd just gone ahead with it and not asked." I remember a similar comment recorded by a pilgrim who asked the Guardian a question and, before answering, the Guardian said to him, "Are you sure you want to know the answer?"

There are cases where you really have to judge for yourself. I remember one case where there was a chappie who was a student of comparative theology, and he was studying for his degree, and he felt it essential for this to read some writings of Covenant-breakers. So he wrote to the House of Justice and said, please may I have permission to read these writings of Covenant-breakers. The House of Justice wrote back and said, but you're not prohibited from reading the writings of Covenant-breakers; you are warned that it's very dangerous, but you're not prohibited from doing it, so we can't give you permission to do it. So he wrote back and said, yes, I realize that, but please I want permission! So the House of Justice wrote again. He just did not want to accept the responsibility. It was a danger to his soul, how could the House of Justice tell him, "You are free to endanger yourself"? There's no prohibition. He had to judge: Do I need to do this, or should I not? So, one must accept these responsibilities.

The exercise of one's mind and the use of one's judgment in obeying a law or instruction are also avenues for divine guidance. I was profoundly impressed by something that the Hand of the Cause Paul Haney once related. He said that sometimes when the Universal House of Justice asked him to undertake a task, he was able at the outset neither to see the wisdom of it, nor how he was to carry it out but, confident in the divine guidance given to the House of Justice, he would set out to do it, and he would find that at every step that he took forward a door would open and the next step would become clear, and he would find at the end that he had been enabled to achieve just what he had been requested to do and he could see the reason for it. This is a perfect example of obedience, faith, wisdom and judgment.

The processes of accepting one's personal responsibility, recognizing one's insufficiency, of seeking and validating an external source of authority and thereby finding the Manifestation of God, of understanding His teachings and of using one's intelligence in implementing them are essential for the development of the individual soul and enable it to fulfill its destiny of coming into harmony with the purpose of God and living in perfect obedience to His designs.

How much more is obedience in this sense essential for the well-being and progress of mankind as a whole. In all parts of the world people are clamoring for freedom, and this striving after freedom and after the material goods of this world is resulting in conflict and war, which are the destroyers of freedom and well-being. Only the guidance of God and Bahá'u'lláh's system of united and willing obedience of individual souls to His guidance can carry mankind from a world of tyranny and oppression across the narrow bridge over the abyss of fragmentation and chaos to the bliss of the Kingdom of God on earth. Then all peoples will recognize the truth of Bahá'u'lláh's words:

> The liberty that profiteth you is to be found nowhere except in complete servitude unto God, the Eternal Truth. Whoso hath tasted of its sweetness will refuse to barter it for all the dominion of earth and heaven.[15]

Violence and the Sexual Abuse of Women and Children*

(*A letter written on behalf of the Universal House of Justice to an individual believer.*)

24th January 1993

Dear Bahá'í Friend,

Further to our letter of 14th November 1991, the Universal House of Justice has now completed its consideration of your letter of 21st September 1991, in which you raised a number of questions pertaining to violence and to the sexual abuse of women and children. We have been instructed to provide the following response to your questions.

As you know, the principle of the oneness of mankind is described in the Bahá'í Writings as the pivot round which all the Teachings of Bahá'u'lláh revolve. It has widespread implications which affect and remold all dimensions of human activity. It calls for a fundamental change in the manner in which people relate to each other, and the eradication of those age-old practices which deny the intrinsic human right of every individual to be treated with consideration and respect.

Within the family setting, the rights of all members must be respected. 'Abdu'l-Bahá has stated

---

* The references, or notes, included in this letter have been placed by the publisher.—Ed.

The integrity of the family bond must be constantly considered and the rights of the individual members must not be transgressed. The rights of the son, the father, the mother—none of them must be transgressed, none of them must be arbitrary.[1]

Just as the son has certain obligations to his father, the father likewise, has certain obligations to his son. The mother, the sister, and other members of the household have their certain prerogatives. All these rights and prerogatives must be conserved.

The use of force by the physically strong against the weak, as a means of imposing one's will and fulfilling one's desires, is a flagrant transgression of the Bahá'í Teachings. There can be no justification for anyone compelling another, through the use of force or through the threat of violence, to do that to which the other person is not inclined. 'Abdu'l-Bahá has written "O ye lovers of God! In this, the cycle of Almighty God, violence and force, constraint and oppression, are one and all condemned."[2] Let those who, driven by their passions or by their inability to exercise discipline in the control of their anger, might be tempted to inflict violence on another human being, be mindful of the condemnation of such disgraceful behavior by the Revelation of Bahá'u'lláh.

Among the signs of moral downfall in the declining social order are the high incidence of violence within the family, the increase in degrading and cruel treatment of spouses and children, and the spread of sexual abuse. It is essential that the members of the community of the Greatest Name take the utmost care not to be drawn into acceptance of such practices because of their prevalence. They must be ever mindful of their obligation to exemplify a new way of life distinguished by its respect for the dignity and rights of all people, by its exalted moral tone, and by its freedom from oppression and from all forms of abuse.

Consultation has been ordained by Bahá'u'lláh as the means by which agreement is to be reached and a collective course of action defined.

It is applicable to the marriage partners and within the family, and indeed, in all areas where believers participate in mutual decisionmaking. It requires all participants to express their opinions with absolute freedom and without apprehension that they will be censured or their views belittled; these prerequisites for success are unattainable if the fear of violence or abuse is present.

A number of your questions pertain to the treatment of women, and are best considered in the light of the principle of the equality of the sexes which is set forth in the Bahá'í Teachings. This principle is far more than the enunciation of admirable ideas; it has profound implications in all aspects of human relations and must be an integral element of Bahá'í domestic and community life. The application of this principle gives rise to changes in habits and practices which have prevailed for many centuries. An example of this is found in the response provided on behalf of Shoghi Effendi to a question whether the traditional practice whereby the man proposes marriage to the woman is altered by the Bahá'í Teachings to permit the woman to issue a marriage proposal to the man; the response is "The Guardian wishes to state that there is absolute equality between the two, and that no distinction or preference is permitted."[3] With the passage of time, during which Bahá'í men and women endeavor to apply more fully the principle of the equality of the sexes, will come a deeper understanding of the far-reaching ramifications of this vital principle. As 'Abdu'l-Bahá has stated "Until the reality of equality between man and woman is fully established and attained, the highest social development of mankind is not possible."[4]

The Universal House of Justice has in recent years urged that encouragement be given to Bahá'í women and girls to participate in greater measure in the social, spiritual and administrative activities of their communities, and has appealed to Bahá'í women to arise and demonstrate the importance of their role in all fields of service to the Faith.

For a man to use force to impose his will on a woman is a serious transgression of the Bahá'í Teachings. 'Abdu'l-Bahá has stated that *[t]he world in the past has been ruled by force, and man has dominated over woman by reason of his more forceful and aggressive qualities both of body and mind. But the balance is already shifting; force is losing its dominance, and mental alertness, intuition, and the spiritual qualities of love and service, in which woman is strong, are gaining ascendancy.*[5]

Bahá'í men have the opportunity to demonstrate to the world around them a new approach to the relationship between the sexes, where aggression and the use of force are eliminated and replaced by cooperation and consultation. The Universal House of Justice has pointed out in response to questions addressed to it that, in a marriage relationship, neither husband nor wife should ever unjustly dominate the other, and that there are times when the husband and the wife should defer to the wishes of the other, if agreement cannot be reached through consultation; each couple should determine exactly under what circumstances such deference is to take place.

From the pen of Bahá'u'lláh Himself has come the following statement on the subject of the treatment of women.

The friends of God must be adorned with the ornament of justice, equity, kindness and love. As they do not allow themselves to be the object of cruelty and transgression, in like manner they should not allow such tyranny to visit the handmaidens of God. He, verily, speaketh the truth and commandeth that which benefitteth His servants and handmaidens. He is the Protector of all in this world and the next.[6]

No Bahá'í husband should ever beat his wife, or subject her to any form of cruel treatment; to do so would be an unacceptable abuse of the marriage relationship and contrary to the Teachings of Bahá'u'lláh.

The lack of spiritual values in society leads to a debasement of the attitudes which should govern the relationship between the sexes, with women being treated as no more than objects for sexual gratification and being denied the respect and courtesy to which all human beings are entitled. Bahá'u'lláh has warned,

"They that follow their lusts and corrupt inclinations, have erred and dissipated their efforts. They indeed, are of the lost."[7] Believers might well ponder the exalted standard of conduct to which they are encouraged to aspire in the statement of Bahá'u'lláh concerning His '*true follower,*' that *"[a]nd if he met the fairest and most comely of women, he would not feel his heart seduced by the least shadow of desire for her beauty. Such an one, indeed, is the creation of spotless chastity. Thus instructeth you the Pen of the Ancient of Days, as bidden by your Lord, the Almighty, the All-Bountiful.*"[8]

One of the most heinous of sexual offences is the crime of rape. When a believer is a victim, she is entitled to the loving aid and support of the members of her community, and she is free to initiate action against the perpetrator under the law of the land should she wish to do so. If she becomes pregnant as a consequence of this assault, no pressure should be brought upon her by the Bahá'í institutions to marry. As to whether she should continue or terminate the pregnancy, it is left to her to decide on the course of action she should follow, taking into consideration medical and other relevant factors, and in the light of the Bahá'í Teachings. If she gives birth to a child as a result of rape, it is left to her discretion whether to seek financial support from the father; however, his claim to any parental rights would, under Bahá'í law, be called into question, in view of the circumstances.

The Guardian has clarified, in letters written on his behalf, that, *"The Bahá'í Faith recognizes the value of the sex impulse'* and that, *"[t]he proper use of the sex instinct is the natural right of every individual, and it is precisely for this very purpose that the institution of marriage has been established.*"[9] In this aspect of the marital relationship, as in all others, mutual consideration and respect should apply. If a Bahá'í woman suffers abuse or is subject to rape by her husband, she has the right to turn to the Spiritual Assembly for assistance and counsel, or to seek legal protection. Such abuse would gravely jeopardize the constitution of the marriage, and could well lead to a condition of irreconcilable antipathy.

You have raised several questions about the treatment of children. It is clear from the Bahá'í Writings that a vital component of the education of children is the exercise of discipline.

Shoghi Effendi has stated, in a letter written on his behalf about the education of children, that

> ... *[d]iscipline of some sort, whether physical, moral or intellectual, is indeed indispensable, and no training can be said to be complete and fruitful if it disregards this element. The child when born is far from being perfect. It is not only helpless, but actually is imperfect, and even is naturally inclined towards evil. He should be trained, his natural inclinations harmonized, adjusted and controlled, and if necessary suppressed or regulated, so as to ensure his healthy physical and moral development. Bahá'í parents cannot simply adopt an attitude of non-resistance towards their children, particularly those who are unruly and violent by nature. It is not even sufficient that they should pray on their behalf. Rather they should endeavor to inculcate, gently and patiently, into their youthful minds such principles ... and teachings of the Cause with such tactful and loving care as would enable them to become "true sons of God" and develop into loyal and intelligent citizens of His Kingdom."*[10]

While the physical discipline of children is an acceptable part of their education and training, such actions are to be carried out *"gently and patiently"* and with *"loving care,"* far removed from the anger and violence with which children are beaten and abused in some parts of the world. To treat children in such an abhorrent manner is a denial of their human rights, and a betrayal of the trust which the weak should have in the strong in a Bahá'í community

It is difficult to imagine a more reprehensible perversion of human conduct than the sexual abuse of children, which finds its most debased form in incest. At a time in the fortunes of humanity when, in the words of the Guardian, *"The perversion of human nature, the degradation of human conduct, the corruption and dissolution of human institutions, reveal themselves ... in their worst and most revolting aspects,"* and when *"the voice of human conscience is stilled,"* when *"the sense of decency and shame is obscured,"*[11] the Bahá'í institutions must be uncompromising and vigilant in their commitment to the protection of the children entrusted to their care, and must not allow either threats or appeals to expediency to divert them from their duty. A parent who is aware that the marriage partner is subjecting children to such sexual abuse should not remain silent, but must take all necessary measures, with the assistance of the Spiritual Assembly or civil authorities if necessary, to bring about an immediate cessation of such grossly immoral behavior, and to promote healing and therapy.

Bahá'u'lláh has placed great emphasis on the duties of parents toward their children, and He has urged children to have gratitude in their hearts for their parents, whose good pleasure they should strive to win as a means of pleasing God Himself. However, He has indicated that under certain circumstances, the parents could be deprived of the right of parenthood as a consequence of their actions. The Universal House of Justice has the right to legislate on this matter. It has decided for the present that all cases should be referred to it in which the conduct or character of a parent appears to render him unworthy of having such parental rights as that of giving consent to marriage. Such questions could arise, for example, when the parent has committed incest, or when the child was conceived as a consequence of rape, and also when a parent consciously fails to protect the child from flagrant sexual abuse.

As humanity passes through the age of transition in its evolution to a world civilization which will be illuminated by spiritual values and will be distinguished by its justice and its unity, the role of the Bahá'í community is clear: it must accomplish a spiritual transformation of its members, and must offer to the world a model of the society destined to come into being through the power of the Revelation of Bahá'u'lláh. Membership in the Bahá'í community is open to all who accept Bahá'u'lláh as the Manifestation of God, and who thereupon embark on the process of changing their conduct and refining their character. It is inevitable that this community will, at times, be subject to delinquent behavior of members whose actions do not conform to the standards of the Teachings. At such times, the institutions of the Faith will not hesitate to apply Bahá'í law with justice and fairness in full confidence that this Divine Law is the means for the true happiness for all concerned.

However, it should be recognized that the ultimate solution to the problems of humanity lies not in penalties and punishments, but rather in spiritual education and illumination. 'Abdu'l-Bahá has written

> It is incumbent upon human society to expend all its forces on the education of the people, and to copiously water men's hearts with the sacred streams that pour down from the Realm of the All-Merciful, and to teach them the manners of Heaven and spiritual ways of life, until every member of the community of man will be schooled, refined, and exalted to such a degree of perfection that the very committing of a shameful act will seem in itself the direst infliction and most agonizing of punishments, and man will fly in terror and seek refuge in God from the very idea of crime, as something far harsher and more grievous than the punishment assigned to it.[12]

It is toward this goal that the community of the Greatest Name is striving, aided and reinforced by the limitless power of the Holy Spirit.

Violence Within Marriage

A Statement by the National Spiritual Assembly of the Bahá'ís of New Zealand

Many of the problems that exist within society also exist within the Bahá'í community. Problems do not vanish from our personal lives just because we have "signed up" as Bahá'ís, or have recognized Bahá'u'lláh as the Manifestation of God for this age. It isn't enough to acknowledge the Divine Physician. We must apply His remedy.

Violence, wherever it occurs, is abhorred in the Bahá'í Faith. As the overwhelming experience within society and within the Bahá'í community is men's violence to women, this is the perspective of the National Spiritual Assembly in preparing this statement. This cannot be taken as indicating any less serious a view being held on other manifestations of violence.

Violence is especially debilitating and reprehensible when it takes place within what is meant to be the safety of one's own home and the sanctity of marriage.

The man who batters his wife, whether with words, fists or feet, may be an ordinary man, who, in the Bahá'í community, comes to Feast, hosts a Holy Day commemoration, participates in Assembly consultation, and on the way home will scream at and abuse his wife for not supporting his views, for smiling at another man, or for talking privately to one of the women. Any behavior of his wife that he can construe as unsupportive, provocative, or independent, may become the "cause" of an outburst. A man who behaves like this—usually only in private—will often say he "just lost control." However, the violent, abusive man usually exercises perfect control over himself; he doesn't behave that way to his work-mates, the police, or other members of the community. He keeps himself well controlled until in the privacy of his home, where his wife and children become the victims of his abuse. Such behavior is seldom the result of a disturbed personality, and it can be challenged, modified and prevented.

What is the effect for the wife and children of a violent man? The woman becomes increasingly fearful, for that is the intention of violence—it is intended to control behavior by producing fear. Such a woman manifests her fear by trying, in turn, to control the environment, so that her husband will have no cause for outbursts. It is a losing battle. The violent, abusive man will always find a reason to express his violence; the house isn't tidy enough; the children were noisy at Feast; she bought a book without his permission; she was elected to the Local Spiritual Assembly.

In addition to trying to control the environment in the home, family and community, the wife of a violent husband will begin to barter her primary responsibility as first educator of their children. In a marriage between equal and mature people, they recognize that the purpose of their marriage is "that from you may appear he who will remember Me amongst My servants."[1] A violent husband is one who insists, overtly through his words, or covertly through his behavior, that his needs come first.

A frightened mother will find, increasingly, that she has to make decisions about the care and well-being of her children which she knows are not good for them, but in an effort to "keep the peace" she will put her violent husband's demands before the rights and needs of her children.

Often lacking transportation ("Oh, he needs the car tonight," or "My husband says the car wouldn't make it to the conference") and money ("I can't afford to give to the Fund"), the wife of a violent husband will become increasingly isolated from the Bahá'í community. If he physically beats her, it will be when the bruises show or she's too sore to move easily that she retreats from the community. If his violence is verbal and psychological, she will increasingly feel unworthy to participate in Bahá'í activities. His verbal abuse will erode her self-confidence. She will become forgetful, indifferent to her appearance, fearful of saying or doing the "wrong" thing. She may become suicidal and anxious about her sanity.

The children from a violent home will usually appear subdued, unwilling to take risks, unable to try new things, and lack spontaneity. The boys will often exhibit violent, anti-social behavior in play as they mirror the same-gender role model. The girls will often be passive and may be unusually helpful, as they mimic their mother's pacifying role. As youth they may be particularly rebellious, not only against their families but maybe against the Bahá'í Faith.

In homes where there is violence, sons often grow up to be violent men and daughters often grow up to be submissive, lacking in self-worth, and end up marrying violent men—thus repeating the cycle.

And what of these violent men in our midst? A few of them know what they are doing is wrong. They love Bahá'u'lláh and desire with all their hearts to align their lives with His teachings. These men are ashamed of their behavior. They will be grateful for the recognition by the Local Spiritual Assembly of their problem. They will readily acknowledge that they are at fault and eagerly pursue a prescribed course of behavior modification.

Most violent men, however, do not know that what they are doing is wrong. They sincerely believe that everyone else is to blame for their problems. Pointing out to these men that what they are doing is wrong, isn't enough. They will merely find ways of disguising their violence, rather than uprooting it from their lives. In His *Will and Testament,* 'Abdu'l-Bahá wrote

Every aggressor deprives himself of God's grace.[2]

Husbands who act violently towards their wives and children are the men 'Abdu'l-Bahá refers to as tyrants.[3] Kindness to such men only encourages their bad behavior.

Kindness cannot be shown the tyrant, the deceiver, or the thief, because, far from awakening them to the error of their ways, it maketh them to continue in their perversity as before.[4]

At this time in our spiritual evolution, we Bahá'ís are still far more influenced by our culture than we are by the Revelation of Bahá'u'lláh. It is the responsibility of the parents within the family, of the Local Spiritual Assembly within the Bahá'í community, and the Bahá'í communities within society, to create an environment in which men's violence within the family is unacceptable and will not be tolerated.

The Universal House of Justice has stated that

. . . no husband should subject his wife to abuse of any kind, whether emotional, mental or physical.[5]

The abuse by husbands of their wives is kept hidden in our Bahá'í communities because of a powerful combination of influences such as isolation; violence which is glorified, amplified and sensationalized by the media; "ownership" of family members; the idea that family violence is between two equals rather than the reality of one weaker partner; economic dependence; and lack of police, legal or community protection. The idea of protection of the Faith has, unfortunately, occasionally been used by well-meaning believers to avoid dealing with violence within a marriage.

Now is the time to face the issues of violence in our own lives and in the lives of those around us. Violence in the Bahá'í community needs to be addressed as it stunts the growth of the human resources of the Faith. It inhibits the proper functioning of our institutions.

The National Spiritual Assembly and the Auxiliary Board Members stand ready to support Local Spiritual Assemblies and the believers at large in their efforts to courageously address and to progressively eliminate the violence in our midst.

Many institutions within New Zealand have recently taken up the challenge not only to address violence, but also to develop policies and procedures by which women can seek help. This will enable women to take their full place in society. Thus it is timely for the National Spiritual Assembly to respond to a need within the Bahá'í community by providing guidelines for Local Spiritual Assemblies. Assemblies will be called upon to provide guidance to men and women within their communities who need protection, challenge and support for change.

Notes

Introduction

1. Dr. Michael Penn, from a talk given at the Green Lake Bahá'í Conference, September 1997.

2. Dr. M. Scott Peck, *The Different Drum: Community Making and Peace*, p. 97.

3. Dr. Thomas G. Banville, *How To Listen—How to Be Heard*, pp. 11, 12, and 18.

4. Bahá'u'lláh, quoted in *The Compilation of Compilations*, 1:93.

5. Ibid.

6. Bahá'u'lláh, *The Seven Valleys and The Four Valleys*, p. 36.

7. 'Abdu'l-Bahá, *Selections from the Writings of 'Abdu'l-Bahá*, no. 160.3.

8. The Universal House of Justice, *The Promise of World Peace: To the Peoples of the World*, p. 28.

9. While I consider that my own healing has sprung from my ever-deepening understanding and embrace of the truths of the Bahá'í Faith, I would like to make clear that it is in no way necessary to be a Bahá'í in order to begin such a healing or to benefit from the balm of the Bahá'í writings. The quotations from the Bahá'í writings that I have included in these pages should support and enhance one's own process of spiritual growth and healing. After all, it is a basic tenet of the Bahá'í teachings that all religions are of the same source, and that ". . . the fundamental purpose of all religions . . . is to bring man closer to God, and to change his character." (Shoghi Effendi, quoted in *The Compilation of Compilations*, 2:434–435.)

Chapter 1/My Own Story

1. For a further discussion of this power, see chapter 4.
2. Bahá'u'lláh, *Gleanings from the Writings of Bahá'u'lláh*, p. 336.
3. From a letter written on behalf of Shoghi Effendi, quoted in *The Compilation of Compilations*, 1:303.
4. Bahá'u'lláh, quoted in *Compilation of Compilations*, 1:248.
5. Bahá'u'lláh, *Kitáb-i-Íqán*, p. 251.
6. 'Abdu'l-Bahá, *Selections from the Writings of 'Abdu'l-Bahá*, no. 97.1.
7. The Báb, in *Bahá'í Prayers: A Selection of Prayers Revealed by Bahá'u'lláh, the Báb, and 'Abdu'l-Bahá*, p. 194.
8. Bahá'u'lláh, *The Hidden Words*, Arabic no. 31.
9. *Compilation*, 1:477.
10. Bahá'u'lláh, *Gleanings*, p. 307.
11. Bahá'u'lláh, *Gleanings*, pp. 306–08.
12. Bahá'u'lláh, *The Seven Valleys*, p. 58.
13. Bahá'u'lláh, quoted in *The Advent of Divine Justice*, p. 32.
14. That is why clergy and priests, who have sexually abused children and women through the centuries, have escaped the consequences of their behavior until the present. Even the concept of reincarnation is tainted with "original sin," when the victim of sexual abuse believes, or is told, it is the consequence of transgressions in a former life. Bahá'u'lláh dispels the notion that we are born evil as He tells us we are created noble, with the potential to follow light or darkness.
15. 'Abdu'l-Bahá, *The Secret of Divine Civilization*, p. 71.
16. Bahá'u'lláh, *The Hidden Words*, Arabic no. 40.
17. 'Abdu'l-Bahá, quoted in *Compilation*, 1:262.
18. 'Abdu'l-Bahá, *Selections from the Writings of 'Abdu'l-Bahá*, no. 111.5 and no. 111.3.

Chapter 2/What is Trauma? Defining the Many Forms of Abuse

1. Bahá'u'lláh, *Gleanings*, p. 99.
2. *The Promulgation of Universal Peace* is an excellent source of information for how to nurture the uneducated, undeveloped, and oppressed.
3. Here, rights equate with powers. Truth and justice are powers,

as is safety, e.g. the power of the fear God, which helps us set limits and boundaries for self and others, thereby creating safety.

4. National Spiritual Assembly of the Bahá'ís of the United States, *Two Wings of a Bird: The Equality of Women and Men*, p. 2.

5. Boundary enmeshment is the uncomfortable and undesirable infringement and control of a person's identity, space, body, sexuality, possessions, emotions, thoughts, and their responsible freedom to express such. It is usually perpetrated by someone who does not recognize their own limits and does not know how to set limits for others. The ultimate remedy for boundary enmeshment requires acknowledgment on the part of the violator and reestablishment of autonomy, privacy, safety, comfort, reciprocity, and unity.

6. Abdication of power is learned helplessness through reward or punishment.

7. Bahá'u'lláh, *The Hidden Words*, Arabic no. 54.

8. Bahá'u'lláh, *The Hidden Words*, Persian no. 74.

9. Bahá'u'lláh, *The Hidden Words*, Persian no. 75.

10. Bahá'u'lláh, *The Kitáb-i-Íqán*, p. 125.

11. See Bahá'u'lláh, *Gleanings*, p. 259 and Bahá'u'lláh, *Tablets of Bahá'u'lláh*, p. 161.

12. "Senses and faculties have been bestowed upon us, to be devoted to the service of the general good; so that we, distinguished above all other forms of life for perceptiveness and reason, should labor at all times and along all lines, whether the occasion be great or small, ordinary or extraordinary, until all mankind are safely gathered into the impregnable stronghold of knowledge." ('Abdu'l-Bahá, *Secret*, p. 3.)

13. ". . . it is a Bahá'í teaching that the spiritual development of the soul requires not merely prayer and meditation, but also active service to one's fellowmen in accordance with the laws and principles of the Revelation of God. The reconstruction of human society and the spiritual advancement of individual souls go hand in hand." (*Messages from the Universal House of Justice, 1963–1986: The Third Epoch of the Formative Age*, no. 397.3.)

Chapter 3/Tyranny, Power, and the Authority of Self

1. Bahá'u'lláh, *The Hidden Words*, Persian no. 64.

2. The Universal House of Justice, *The Promise of World Peace*, p. 23.

3. Ibid., p. 28.

4. Ibid.

5. Bahá'u'lláh, *Tablets*, p. 84.
6. Bahá'u'lláh, *Tablets*, p. 85.
7. Bahá'u'lláh, *Gleanings*, p. 218.
8. *Gleanings*, p. 219.
9. 'Abdu'l-Bahá, *Foundations of World Unity*, p. 9.
10. *Two Wings of a Bird*, p. 7.
11. N. Josefowitz, *Paths to Power*, p. 4.
12. "Violence and the Sexual Abuse of Women and Children," a letter written on behalf of the Universal House of Justice to an individual believer, January 24, 1993 printed in *The American Bahá'í*, November 23, 1993 (vol. 24, no. 7), pp. 10–11. The entire letter can be found in Appendix II, pp. 177–184.
13. The entire text of Ian Semple's talk on "Obedience" can be found in Appendix I, pp. 157–176.
14. Ian Semple, from an address titled "Obedience" presented in connection with the Spiritual Enrichment Program at the Bahá'í World Center, July 26, 1991.
15. Ibid.

Chapter 4/The Powers of the Authority of Self

1. Bahá'u'lláh, *Gleanings*, p. 200.
2. Bahá'u'lláh, *Seven Valleys*, p. 55.
3. The Báb, *Selections from the Writings of the Báb*, p. 213.
4. The Báb, *Bahá'í Prayers*, p. 22.
5. 'Abdu'l-Bahá, *Some Answered Questions*, p. 247.
6. Bahá'u'lláh, *Gleanings*, p. 336.
7. Bahá'u'lláh, *The Kitáb-i-Aqdas*, ¶1.
8. Bahá'u'lláh, *Gleanings*, p. 143.
9. Bahá'u'lláh, *Gleanings*, p. 268.
10. Quotations for the power of discernment are from *Gleanings*, p. 160; *Tablets*, p. 105, p. 137–138; and *Selections from the Writings of the Báb*, p. 124.
11. *Tablets*, p. 66.
12. *Tablets*, p. 151.
13. Further quotations on wisdom can be found in *Epistle to the Son of the Wolf*, p. 12, and *Tablets*, p. 239.
14. *Tablets*, p. 126.

15. *Gleanings*, p. 262.

16. *Tablets*, p. 63.

17. See also *The Hidden Words*, Arabic no. 24 and *The Hidden Words*, Arabic no. 43.

18. *Tablets*, p. 194.

19. The power of understanding is noted in *Epistle*, p. 41; *Bahá'í World Faith*, p. 339; and *Some Answered Questions*, p. 221.

20. 'Abdu'l-Bahá, *Secret*, p. 11.

21. 'Abdu'l-Bahá, *Bahá'í Prayers*, p. 113.

22. The power of perception is noted in *Tablets*, p. 75; *Selections from the Writings of the Báb*, p. 21–22; *Tablets*, p. 35; *Bahá'í Prayers*, p. 193; and *Some Answered Questions*, p. 217.

23. *Gleanings*, p. 326–327.

24. *Selections from the Writings of 'Abdu'l-Bahá*, no. 36.3.

25. From a letter written on behalf of Shoghi Effendi to an individual believer, *Compilation*, 2:18–19.

26. 'Abdu'l-Bahá, *Bahá'í Prayers*, p. 138.

27. 'Abdu'l-Bahá, quoted in *The World Order of Bahá'u'lláh*, p. 139.

28. *Tablets*, p. 164.

29. Quotations that relate to identity can be found in *Tablets*, p. 156; *The Hidden Words*, Persian nos. 72 and 27; *The Hidden Words*, Arabic no. 3; *Some Answered Questions*, pp. 246–247; *Gleanings*, p. 218; *The Kitáb-i-Íqán*, p. 240; and *Bahá'í Prayers*, p. 111.

30. Belenky, Clinchy, Goldberger, and Tarule, *Women's Ways of Knowing*, pp. 15, 25, 28, and 39.

31. *Tablets*, p. 62.

32. *Tablets*, p. 199.

33. There are several mentions of the power of utterance: *Gleanings*, pp. 92, 164, 265, 278, 303, and 312; and *The Kitáb-i-Íqán*, p. 194; *Tablets*, pp. 57, 73, 84, and 239.

34. 'Abdu'l-Bahá, *Paris Talks*, no. 2.1

35. 'Abdu'l-Bahá, *The Promulgation of Universal Peace*, p. 291.

36. Further quotations referring to the power of reasoning can be found in *Secret*, pp. 3 and 60; and *Paris Talks*, no. 55.2.

37. *Bahá'í World Faith*, p. 383.

38. *Gleanings*, p. 217; and *The Proclamation of Bahá'u'lláh*, p. 114.

39. *Tablets of Abdul-Baha Abbas*, vol. 1, p. 195.

40. *Bahá'í Prayers*, p. 15.

41. *Promulgation*, pp. 90–91.

42. Further references to the power of inner vision can be found in *Bahá'í World Faith*, pp. 266 and 304.

43. For example, see the "Fire Tablet" (*Bahá'í Prayers*, pp. 214–220); His anguish at the death of His son, Mírzá Mihdí, the Purest Branch (*Prayers and Meditations*, pp. 34–35); or the lamentation in His voice while at the mercy of God's enemies (*Prayers*, p. 39). Because of the betrayal He felt by His brother, Mírzá Yaḥyá, He speaks of "writhing in anguish upon the dust, like unto a fish," beseeching God to deliver Him. He also reveals how He wept for Mírzá Yaḥyá (*The Kitáb-i-Aqdas*, ¶184). See also *Gleanings*, pp. 118 and 169.

44. 'Abdu'l-Bahá, *Some Answered Questions*, p. 300.

45. Alice Miller, *Thou Shalt Not Be Aware* (New York: Farrar, Straus, and Giroux, 1984).

46. *Promulgation*, pp. 280–281.

47. Further references to the power of knowledge can be found in *The Kitáb-i-Íqán*, pp. 140 and 185.

48. *Some Answered Questions*, p. 248.

49. Further references to the power of will can be found in *Gleanings*, pp. 94, 120, 143, 149, 164, 209, 337, and 338; *Tablets*, p. 23; *Bahá'í World Faith*, p. 339; *The Hidden Words*, Persian nos. 19 and 31; *Prayers*, pp. 108 and 241; and *Some Answered Questions*, pp. 248–250.

50. See also *Some Answered Questions*, pp. 187 and 210.

51. 'Abdu'l-Bahá, in *August Forel and the Bahá'í Faith*, pp. 11–12.

52. *Promulgation*, p. 49.

53. *Tablets*, p. 72.

54. Further references to the power of reflection can be found in *Gleanings*, p. 262 and *Tablets*, p. 72.

55. *Bahá'í World Faith*, p. 244.

56. Ibid.

57. Further references to intellectual investigation can be found in *Promulgation*, p. 180, and *Some Answered Questions*, p. 218.

58. Paulo Freire, *Pedogogy of the Oppressed*, p. 58.

59. *The Promise of World Peace*, p. 28.

60. *The Promulgation of Universal Peace*, p. 49.

61. The Universal House of Justice, quoted in *The Compilation of Compilations*, 1:111.

62. *Bahá'í Prayers*, p. 210.

63. 'Abdu'l-Bahá, *Some Answered Questions*, p. 210.

64. 'Abdu'l-Bahá, quoted in *Bahá'í Prayers*, p. 152.

Chapter 5/Boundaries, Anger, and Cognitive Distortions: Stumbling Blocks for Those Recovering from Trauma

1.   Many people are familiar with a definition of "developmentally delayed" as not having completed the developmental stages of childhood, whether emotional, mental, or physical. A more expanded definition of "developmentally delayed" would be: development of powers that make up authority of self has been arrested at the age-appropriate times they should have been granted incrementally by authority as the child became capable or responsible. Disempowerment was thought to be necessary either because of inherent disability on the part of the child or because authority was unjust or bereft of the knowledge necessary to assist the child or adult.

2.   Bahá'u'lláh, *Gleanings*, p. 11.

3.   Dr. David D. Burns, *Feeling Good: the New Mood Therapy*, p. 40.

4.   Bahá'u'lláh, *The Kitáb-i-Aqdas*, ¶125.

5.   *The Kitáb-i-Aqdas*, ¶123.

6.   *The Kitáb-i-Aqdas*, ¶3, 4, and 5.

7.   *The Kitáb-i-Aqdas*, ¶2.

8.   Bahá'u'lláh, *Tablets*, p. 63.

9.   John Bradshaw, *Creating Love*, p. 33.

10.   'Abdu'l-Bahá, *Selections from the Writings of 'Abdu'l-Bahá*, no. 205.4.

11.   'Abdu'l-Bahá, *Selections from the Writings of 'Abdu'l-Bahá*, no. 19.3.

12.   'Abdu'l-Bahá, *Selections from the Writings of 'Abdu'l-Bahá*, no. 97.1.

13.   The Báb, *Selections from the Writings of the Báb*, p. 133.

14.   Letter written on the behalf of the Universal House of Justice to an individual believer, January 24, 1993, printed in *The American Bahá'í*, November 23, 1993 (vol. 24, no. 17), p. 10.

15.   Bahá'u'lláh, *The Hidden Words*, Persian no. 43.

16.   You can begin by keeping a daily log or journal of passing events, as well as your physical distress, vague memories, and dreams, including your ability or inability to sleep at night.

17.   Bahá'u'lláh, *Tablets*, p. 120.

18.   Bahá'u'lláh, *Gleanings*, p. 265.

19. 'Abdu'l-Bahá, *Selections from the Writings of 'Abdu'l-Bahá*, no. 9.3.

20. Matthew McKay, Peter D. Rogers, and Judith McKay, *When Anger Hurts*, pp. 3–5.

21. Deidre Laiken and A. Schneider, *Listen to Me, I'm Angry: A Book for Teenagers*, pp. 31–35.

22. Adele Mayer, *Sex Offenders*, pp. 19–28.

23. I designated "feeling" anger, not "behaving" in anger. They are two different concepts. Feeling anger is a component of authority of self which considers appropriate ways of consciously electing moral choices (again, that is using the cognitive power). Behaving in anger is an action which can be condemned because it is usually inappropriate, futile, and ineffective or destructive.

24. *Promulgation*, p. 168.

25. Virginia Satir and John Banmen, *Satir Model*, p. 62.

26. Bahá'u'lláh, "The Fire Tablet," *Bahá'í Prayers*, p. 217.

27. *Selections from the Writings of 'Abdu'l-Bahá*, nos. 24.1–24.2.

28. Bahá'u'lláh, *The Hidden Words*, Arabic no. 63.

29. Burns, *Feeling Good*, p. 40.

30. *Compilation*, 1:379.

31. Bahá'u'lláh, *The Hidden Words*, Arabic no. 69.

32. Bahá'u'lláh, *Compilation*, 1:379.

33. Bahá'u'lláh, *The Hidden Words*, Persian no. 64.

34. Bahá'u'lláh, *The Hidden Words*, Persian no. 65.

35. Bahá'u'lláh, *The Hidden Words*, Persian no. 43.

Chapter 6/ Aiding the Traumatized: How Communities and Individuals Can Help

1. *Gleanings*, p. 200.

2. *Promulgation*, p. 291.

3. *Promulgation*, p. 315.

4. Ian Semple to Phyllis Peterson, personal correspondence, November 11, 1994.

5. Ibid. Passage from the Holy Bible appears in Matthew 18:6.

6. Ian Semple to Phyllis Peterson, personal correspondence, November 11, 1994.

7. *Compilation*, 1:477.

8. "Mental Health: Does Therapy Help You?" *Consumer Reports*, (November 1995): 735.

9. From a letter written on behalf of the Guardian to an individual believer, April 12, 1948, *Lights of Guidance*, p. 225.

10. From a letter written on behalf of the Guardian to an individual believer, *Unfolding Destiny*, p. 462.

11. Ibid.

12. *The Hidden Words*, Persian no. 80.

13. *The Hidden Words*, Persian no. 82.

14. Letter written on behalf of the Universal House of Justice, June 5, 1985, to a National Spiritual Assembly, quoted in *Developing Distinctive Bahá'í Communities*, no. 15.25.

15. "Whoso wisheth to recite this prayer, let him stand up and turn unto God, and, as he standeth in his place, let him gaze to the right and to the left, as if awaiting the mercy of his Lord, the Most Merciful, the Compassionate." *Bahá'í Prayers*, p. 7.

16. References to this power can be found in *Gleanings*, pp. 17, 82, and 340; *Tablets*, p. 252; and *Prayers*, p. 109.

17. *Epistle*, pp. 44–45. More examples can be found in *Gleanings*, pp. 67 and 335; *Tablets*, pp. 103, 220, and 236; and *The Kitáb-i-Íqán*, pp. 108 and 124.

18. The Universal House of the Justice, "To the Bahá'ís of the World: Riḍván Message, 153 B.E.," quoted in *The Four Year Plan: Messages of the Universal House of Justice*, no. 3.22.

19. Quotations regarding the power of response can be found in *The Kitáb-i-Íqán*, p. 235; *Prayers*, pp. 113 and 287; *Tablets*, pp. 176, 232, and 238; and *Gleanings*, pp. 236 and 339.

20. Examples of the power of attention can be found in *Tablets*, pp. 90, 200, and 256; *Epistle*, p. 9; *Gleanings*, pp. 13, 103, 205, 241, and 272; *The Hidden Words*, Persian no. 11; and *The Kitáb-i-Íqán*, pp. 181 and 202.

21. "Fragmenting" of perception is the condition of being so fearful and disempowered or self-willed and individualistic in one's reality that one can not admit the reality of others in order to achieve oneness in consultation. It can be witnessed in alienation, divisiveness, preconceptions, expectations, prejudices, and rigid roles. It is when we stop regarding ourselves as separate, independent entities that we will be prepared to receive the reality of another as valid and whole, as undivided from ours, even in mental illness. And from this wholeness will flow an orderly unfolding of knowledge.

22. To "paraphrase" is to reflect through language, lifting into their attention the content, context, and feelings of what you have heard verbally or seen physically that is important to their understanding of their reality. The language we use with the traumatized can either

sustain fragmentation or promote oneness. Be assured that one will cause confusion and repel them away from our "help," and the other will draw them to us, to the writings, and into unity.

23. *Bahá'í Prayers*, p. 111.

24. *Bahá'í Prayers*, p. 103.

25. Earl A. Grollman, *Suicide: Prevention, Intervention, Postvention*, p. 67.

26. Grollman, *Suicide*, pp. 77–87.

27. The names in this story have been changed to protect the privacy of the individuals who were gracious enough to allow me to share this story.

28. Bahá'í International Community, "The Family in a World Community," November 1993, p. 1.

29. *Bahá'í Prayers*, p. 105.

30. The Universal House of Justice, quoted in *Local Spiritual Assembly Handbook*, pp. 260–261.

31. *Local Spiritual Assembly Handbook*, pp. 260.

32. Letter written on the behalf of the Universal House of Justice to an individual believer, January 24, 1993, printed in *The American Bahá'í*, p. 10.

33. Letter written on behalf of the Universal House of Justice to the National Spiritual Assembly of Australia, dated April 12, 1990, quoted in *Local Spiritual Assembly Handbook*, p. 261.

34. Ibid., p. 262.

35. Ibid., pp. 262–263.

36. *Local Spiritual Assembly Handbook*, p. 263.

37. There are a multitude of support groups, some connected to official shelters, safe homes for children, as well as AA and Alanon.

38. Alyce Blue to Phyllis Peterson, personal correspondence, n.d.

39. Dr. David D. Burns, *Feeling Good: the New Mood Therapy*, p. 40.

Chapter 7/The Current Perpetrators of Abuse

1. Naomi I. Brill, *Working With People: The Helping Process*, p. 136.

2. Oscar Arrambide to Phyllis Peterson, personal correspondence, n.d.

3. *Developing Distinctive Bahá'í Communities*, 15.26.

4. *Local Spiritual Assembly Handbook*, pp. 263–264.

5. 'Abdu'l-Bahá, *Paris Talks*, no. 47.5.
6. Bahá'u'lláh, quoted in *The Advent of Divine Justice*, p. 24.
7. 'Abdu'l-Bahá, quoted in *Bahá'í World Faith*, p. 412.
8. Oscar Arrambide to Phyllis Peterson, personal correspondence, n.d.
9. Letter written on the behalf of the Universal House of Justice to an individual believer, January 24, 1993, printed in *The American Bahá'í*, November 23, 1993, p. 10.
10. Bahá'u'lláh, *Gleanings*, p. 265.
11. Janet Cullen Tanaka, "Counseling Members of the Bahá'í Faith Involved in Domestic Violence," *Bahá'í Studies Notebook: The Divine Institution of Marriage, III*, p. 146.
12. *The Kitáb-i-Aqdas*, p. 201.
13. *Tablets of Bahá'u'lláh*, p. 221.
14. *The Kitáb-i-Aqdas*, ¶107.
15. *The Kitáb-i-Aqdas*, p. 222.
16. The Universal House of Justice, to an individual believer, January 24, 1993, printed in *The American Bahá'í*, November 23, 1993, p. 11.
17. "Assembly Must Report Child Abuse to Authorities," *The American Bahá'í*, April 9, 1994 (Vol. 25, no. 5), p. 9.
18. *Tablets of Bahá'u'lláh*, pp. 219–220.

Appendix I/Obedience

1. Bahá'u'lláh, *Gleanings*, p. 207.
2. Bahá'u'lláh, *The Hidden Words*, Arabic no. 2.
3. Bahá'u'lláh, *Gleanings*, p. 105.
4. Ibid., p. 98.
5. Ibid., pp. 105–106.
6. The Báb, *Selections from the Writings of the Báb*, p. 124.
7. Ibid.
8. Bahá'u'lláh, *Prayers and Meditations*, p. 149.
9. The Holy Bible, Job 38:1–7.
10. Bahá'u'lláh, *Gleanings*, p. 337.
11. Bahá'u'lláh, *Tablets*, p. 68.
12. 'Abdu'l-Bahá, in *Bahá'í World Faith*, p. 383.
13. Shoghi Effendi, *Compilation*, 1:303.
14. Bahá'u'lláh, *Tablets*, p. 36.
15. Bahá'u'lláh, *The Kitáb-i-Aqdas*, ¶125.

Appendix II/Violence and the Sexual Abuse of Children

1. 'Abdu'l-Bahá, *Promulgation*, p. 168.
2. 'Abdu'l-Bahá, *Selections from the Writings of 'Abdu'l-Bahá*, no. 129.11.
3. From a letter written on the behalf of Shoghi Effendi, n.d., previously unpublished.
4. 'Abdu'l-Bahá, *Promulgation*, p. 76.
5. 'Abdu'l-Bahá, *Compilation*, 2:368–69.
6. Bahá'u'lláh, *Compilation*, 2:369.
7. Bahá'u'lláh, *Compilation*, 2:327–28.
8. Bahá'u'lláh, *Gleanings*, p. 118–19.
9. From a letter written on the behalf of Shoghi Effendi, *Compilation*, 1:56.
10. From a letter written on the behalf of Shoghi Effendi, quoted in *Compilation*, 1:303.
11. Shoghi Effendi, *The World Order of Bahá'u'lláh*, p. 187.
12. From a previously unpublished Tablet of 'Abdu'l-Bahá.

Appendix III/Violence Within Marriage: A Statement by the National Spiritual Assembly of the Bahá'ís of New Zealand

1. Bahá'u'lláh, in *Bahá'í Prayers*, p. 105.
2. 'Abdu'l-Bahá, *Will and Testament of 'Abdu'l-Bahá*, p. 13.
3. Tyrant: "Person exercising power or authority arbitrarily or cruelly." (From the *Concise Oxford Dictionary*.)
4. 'Abdu'l-Bahá, *Selections from the Writings of 'Abdu'l-Bahá*, no. 138. 1.
5. The Universal House of Justice, *Compilation*, 2:459.

Bibliography

Works of Bahá'u'lláh

Epistle to the Son of the Wolf. Translated by Shoghi Effendi. 1st ps ed. Wilmette, Ill.: Bahá'í Publishing Trust, 1988.

Gleanings from the Writings of Bahá'u'lláh. Translated by Shoghi Effendi. 1st ps ed. Wilmette, Ill.: Bahá'í Publishing Trust, 1983.

The Hidden Words. Translated by Shoghi Effendi. Wilmette, Ill.: Bahá'í Publishing Trust, 1939.

The Kitáb-i-Aqdas: The Most Holy Book. 1st ps ed. Wilmette, Ill.: Bahá'í Publishing Trust, 1993.

The Kitáb-i-Íqán: The Book of Certitude. Translated by Shoghi Effendi. 1st ps ed. Wilmette, Ill.: Bahá'í Publishing Trust, 1983.

Prayers and Meditations. Translated by Shoghi Effendi. 1st ps ed. Wilmette, Ill.: Bahá'í Publishing Trust, 1987.

The Proclamation of Bahá'u'lláh to the Kings and Leaders of the World. Haifa: Bahá'í World Centre, 1972.

The Seven Valleys and The Four Valleys. New Ed. Translated by Marzieh Gail and Ali-Kuli Khan. Wilmette, Ill.: Bahá'í Publishing Trust, 1991.

Tablets of Bahá'u'lláh revealed after the Kitáb-i-Aqdas. Compiled by the Research Department of the Universal House of Justice. Translated by Habib Taherzadeh et al. 1st ps ed. Wilmette, Ill.: Bahá'í Publishing Trust, 1988.

Works of the Báb

Selections from the Writings of the Báb. Compiled by the Research Department of the Universal House of Justice. Translated by Habib Taherzadeh et al. Haifa: Bahá'í World Centre, 1976.

Works of 'Abdu'l-Bahá

Foundations of World Unity: Compiled from Addresses and Tablets of 'Abdu'l-Bahá. Wilmette, Ill.: Bahá'í Publishing Trust, 1972.

Paris Talks: Addresses Given by 'Abdu'l-Bahá in Paris in 1911. 12ᵗʰ ed. London: Bahá'í Publishing Trust, 1995.

The Promulgation of Universal Peace: Talks Delivered by 'Abdu'l-Bahá during His Visit to the United States and Canada in 1912. Compiled by Howard MacNutt. 2ⁿᵈ ed. Wilmette, Ill.: Bahá'í Publishing Trust, 1982.

The Secret of Divine Civilization. Translated by Marzieh Gail and Ali-Kuli Khan. 1ˢᵗ ps ed. Wilmette, Ill.: Bahá'í Publishing Trust, 1990.

Selections from the Writings of 'Abdu'l-Bahá. Compiled by the Research Department of the Universal House of Justice. Translated by a Committee at the Bahá'í World Centre and Marzieh Gail. 1ˢᵗ ps ed. Wilmette, Ill.: Bahá'í Publishing Trust, 1997.

Some Answered Questions. Compiled and translated by Laura Clifford Barney. 1ˢᵗ ps ed. Wilmette, Ill.: Bahá'í Publishing Trust, 1984.

Tablets of Abdul-Baha Abbas. 3 vols. New York: Bahai Publishing Society, 1909–16.

Will and Testament of 'Abdu'l-Bahá. Wilmette, Ill.: Bahá'í Publishing Trust, 1944.

Works of Shoghi Effendi

The Advent of Divine Justice. 1ˢᵗ ps ed. Wilmette,Ill.: Bahá'í Publishing Trust, 1990.

The Unfolding Destiny of the British Bahá'í Community: The Messages from the Guardian of the Bahá'í Faith to the Bahá'ís of the British Isles. London: Bahá'í Publishing Trust, 1981.

The World Order of Bahá'u'lláh: Selected Letters. New ed. Wilmette, Ill.: Bahá'í Publishing Trust, 1991.

Works of the Universal House of Justice

Messages from the Universal House of Justice, 1963–1986: The Third

Epoch of the Formative Age. Compiled by Geoffry W. Marks. Wilmette, Ill.: Bahá'í Publishing Trust, 1996.
The Promise of World Peace: To the Peoples of the World. Wilmette, Ill.: Bahá'í Publishing Trust, 1985.
The Four Year Plan: Messages of the Universal House of Justice. Riviera Beach, Fl.: Palabra Publications, 1996.

Compilations from the Bahá'í Writings

Bahá'u'lláh and 'Abdu'l-Bahá. *Bahá'í World Faith: Selected Writings of Bahá'u'lláh and 'Abdu'l-Bahá.* 2d ed. Wilmette, Ill.: Bahá'í Publishing Trust, 1976.
Bahá'u'lláh, the Báb, and 'Abdu'l-Bahá. *Bahá'í Prayers: A Selection of Prayers Revealed by Bahá'u'lláh, the Báb, and 'Abdu'l-Bahá.* New ed. Wilmette, Ill.: Bahá'í Publishing Trust, 1991.
The Compilation of Compilations: Prepared by the Universal House of Justice 1963–1990. 2 vols. Australia: Bahá'í Publications Australia, 1991.

Other Works

['Abdu'l-Bahá and Forel, Auguste.] *Auguste Forel and the Bahá'í Faith.* Translated by Hélène Neri. Commentary by Peter Mühlschlegel. Oxford: George Ronald, 1978.
Association for Bahá'í Studies. *Bahá'í Studies Notebook: The Divine Institution of Marriage.* Ottawa, Ont.: Association for Bahá'í Studies, 1983.
Bahá'í International Community. "The Family in a World Community." New York: Bahá'í International Community, n.d.
Banville, Dr. Thomas G. *How to Listen—How to Be Heard.* Chicago: Nelson-Hall, 1978.
Belenky, Mary Field, Clinchy, Blythe McVicker, Goldberger, Nancy Rule, and Tarule, Jill Mattuck. *Women's Ways of Knowing: The Development of Self, Voice and Mind.* United States: Basic Books, 1986.
Bradshaw, John E. *Creating Love.* New York: Bantam Books, 1990.
—————. *Bradshaw On: Healing the Shame That Binds You.* Deerfield Beach, Fl.: Health Communications, Inc., 1988.

Brill, Naomi. *Working With People: The Helping Process.* White Plains, NY: Longman Publishing Group, 1980.

Burns, Dr. David. *Feeling Good: The New Mood Therapy.* New York: William Morrow and Company, 1980.

Developing Distinctive Bahá'í Communities: Guidelines for Spiritual Assemblies. Compiled by the Office of Assembly Development. Rev. ed. Evanston, Ill.: National Spiritual Assembly of the Bahá'ís of the United States, 1998.

Esslemont, J. E. *Bahá'u'lláh and the New Era: An Introduction to the Bahá'í Faith.* 5ᵗʰ rev. ed. Wilmette, Ill.: Bahá'í Publishing Trust, 1980.

Freire, Paulo. *Pedogogy of the Oppressed.* New York: The Continuum Publishing, 1970.

Grollman, Earl A. *Suicide: Prevention, Intervention, and Postvention.* Boston: Beacon Press, 1988.

Josefowitz, N. *Paths to Power.* La Port, IN: Addison Wesley, Longman, Inc., 1980.

Laiken, Deidre and Schneider, A. *Listen to Me, I'm Angry: A Book for Teenagers.* New York: Lothrop, Lee and Shepard, 1980.

McKay, Matthew, Rogers, Peter D., and McKay, Judith. *When Anger Hurts.* Oakland, Ca.: New Harbinger Publications, 1989.

Mayer, Adele. *Sex Offenders.* Holmes Beach, Fl.: Learning Publications, Inc. 1988.

Miller, Alice. *For Your Own Good: Hidden Cruelty in Child-Rearing and the Roots of Violence.* Translated by Hildegarde and Hunter Hannum. New York: Farrar, Straus, and Giroux, 1983.

———. *Thou Shalt Not Be Aware: Society's Betrayal of the Child.* Translated by Hildegarde and Hunter Hannum. New York: Farrar, Straus, and Giroux, 1984.

National Spiritual Assembly of the Bahá'ís of Australia. *Local Spiritual Assembly Handbook.* 3ʳᵈ ed. Mona Vale, Australia: Bahá'í Publications Australia, 1996.

National Spiritual Assembly of the Bahá'ís of the United States. *Two Wings of a Bird: The Equality of Women and Men, A Statement by the National Spiritual Assembly of the Bahá'ís of the United States.* Wilmette, Ill.: Bahá'í Publishing Trust, 1997.

Peck, M. Scott. *The Different Drum: Community Making and Peace.* New York: Simon and Schuster, 1987.

Satir, Virginia and John Banmen. *Satir Model.* Palo Alto, Calif.: Science and Behavior Books, 1991.

Index